DEEP CHANGE

DEEP CHANGE

*Discovering
the Leader
Within*

ROBERT E. QUINN

Jossey-Bass Publishers
San Francisco

Substantial discounts on bulk quantities of Jossey-Bass books are available to corporations, professional associations, and other organizations. For details and discount information, contact the special sales department at Jossey-Bass Inc., Publishers (415) 433-1740; Fax (800) 605-2665.

For sales outside the United States, please contact your local Simon & Schuster International Office.

Jossey-Bass Web address: http://www.josseybass.com

 Manufactured in the United States of America on Lyons Falls Turin Book. This paper is acid-free and 100 percent totally chlorine-free.

Library of Congress Cataloging-in-Publication Data

Quinn, Robert E.
    Deep change : discovering the leader within / Robert E. Quinn.
        p.   cm. — (Jossey-Bass business and management series)
    Includes bibliographical references and index.
    ISBN 0-7879-0244-6
    1. Organizational change—Management. 2. Leadership. I. Title.
II. Series.
HD58.8.Q56   1996
658.4'06—dc20   96-22674

FIRST EDITION
HB Printing   10 9 8 7 6 5 4 3

The Jossey-Bass
Business & Management Series

This book is dedicated to Reed H. Bradford, Marion D. Hanks, and Orin R. Woodbury, three internally driven people who understood excellence, modeled integrity, and helped me, at an early point in my life, understand the process of deep change. Those early investments are deeply appreciated.

Contents

Preface

Many years ago, I was walking home from high school basketball practice when I spotted a *Time* magazine in the local drugstore window. On the cover was Oscar Robertson, who, after a spectacular basketball career at the University of Cincinnati, was in his first year in the National Basketball Association. I had read a lot about the "Big O" and considered him a bit of a hero. Lured into the store, I bought a copy of the magazine and quickly read the article.

The article described Robertson as the first complete player, the perfect athlete who excelled at every part of the game. The article argued that Robertson's presence and his excellence in the National Basketball Association were changing the nature of the NBA. It was not the first time I had read about his changing the context in which he operated. In college, he had received extensive coverage in the media, and he was often deeply resented when his team arrived on southern campuses. There was almost always taunting and catcalls. The most frequent was "Skycap," a slightly veiled way of saying, "Nigger, you don't belong here." Robertson, of course, did belong, and his athletic excellence was so potent that even the most bigoted audience had to appreciate the beauty and brilliance of his performance. In that sense, Oscar was not only a great athlete, he was also a social change agent.

What I remember most from the *Time* article, however, was the description of a very small incident that occurred as Robertson's college team was leaving a game. A university publicity person was casually dribbling a basketball on the cement pavement. Robertson was appalled and approached him, saying, "You'll ruin that ball. You'll rub off the grain and throw it off balance."

The article went on to explain Robertson's background. His family could not afford to buy him a basketball, so he collected rocks and cans and spent hours shooting these objects at a bent rim in the local playground. This vivid picture occupies a special place in my teenage memories. Though I never had any of Robertson's talents, I shared his dream. More than anything else, I wanted to be a great basketball player, and I spent much of my youth shooting lopsided balls at bent rims. At fourteen, I earned the money to buy a good ball that would not go lopsided. I slept with that ball and washed it every time I used it. People made fun of me, but they truly did not understand about basketballs, not really, not deeply.

Oscar and I shared a common understanding. We both had reverence for the same object because we both understood its potential. When a basketball is placed in the hands of a master, like Oscar, magical things can happen. The talented master has the ability to become a leader who induces change. The leader can transform separate individuals into cohesive teams. So linked, these individuals can communicate without words. They can capture the imagination of larger communities, enticing them to dream new dreams. Even the most tightly held prejudice, in some populations, can be muted. In the end, excellence is infectious.

Purpose of the Book

Deep Change assumes that one person can change the larger system or organization in which he or she exists. In this sense, each of us is a potential Oscar Robertson. This book, however, is not about basketballs or other specific tools. It is about the process of transformation or deep change. Confronting and experiencing a deep personal or organizational change is a difficult decision. When we have successfully experienced a deep change, it inspires us to encourage others to undergo a similar experience.

We are all potential change agents. As we discipline our talents, we deepen our perceptions about what is possible. We develop a reverence for the tools and the relationships that surround us. We then bring a discipline to our visions and grow in integrity. Life becomes more meaningful. We become empowered and empowering to our context. Having experienced deep change in ourselves, we are able to bring deep change to the systems around us.

We live in a tumultuous time. Change is everywhere, and we are surrounded by circumstances that seem to demand more than we can deliver. We are all regularly lured into playing the role of the powerless victim or the passive observer. In such roles, we become detached, and our sense of meaning decays. We look at everything in a superficial way. We see little potential and have little reverence. To choose to play either of these roles is to choose meaninglessness or the slow death of the self.

We have always been embedded in a dilemma. We have always had to agonize over the choice between making deep change or accepting slow death. Today, however, the dilemma is more blatant. As soon as we find meaning and equilibrium, it is distorted. We must continually choose between deep change or slow death. This book is about confronting that dilemma.

Who Should Read This Book

All of us, at some point in life, get overwhelmed and disconnected and feel that our life lacks meaning. We realize that we need to do something to alter our present situation but lack the motivation and inspiration to do so. We also recognize that we want to influence and change the behavior of others. If you must face up to the need to change and do not quite know how to get through the process, this book is for you.

Many of the stories in this volume come from the world of

business. This book, however, is not just for people who work in business organizations. It is for all who want to make a difference and yearn to be internally driven leaders who encourage and motivate the people around them.

Relationship to *Beyond Rational Management*

Some of you may be familiar with my book *Beyond Rational Management* or my other works featuring the competing values model. If so, you may feel that this book is not connected with that line of work, but actually it is. The competing values model offers four competing ways to see the world. It helps people understand that many of the most perplexing issues are not trade-offs between bad and bad but between good and good.

The model helps increase awareness and provides a wider range of choices. The model does not, however, provide a right answer. For people with responsibility in the world, the most important questions do not have simple solutions. How, then, does someone make a decision? Our capacity to face uncertainty and function in times of stress and anxiety is linked with our self-confidence, and our level of confidence is linked with our sense of increasing integrity. We are all affected by technical competence or political acumen, but we are more deeply influenced by moral power. In the end, the latter is the ultimate source of power. This book is about the process of becoming an internally driven leader who is able to draw on his or her own ultimate source of power.

Organization of the Book

This book explores the process of deep change and the development of internally driven leadership. Part One defines deep change and explains what it means to "walk naked into the land of uncertainty." It helps us understand how the "deep change or slow death dilemma" affects every part of our lives. Part Two focuses on the confrontation of the deep change or slow death dilemma and the necessity for first transforming self. A number of insights provide guidance for finding the alignment of self within the surrounding environment. Part Three suggests that an internally driven leader views the world differently. Here insight is gained into how to take the transformational perspective, a position of reverence for the moral core of the community. Finally, Part Four focuses on vision, risk, and the creation of excellence. This part will challenge you to find, develop, evaluate, and communicate a vision that will move others to their highest levels of excellence.

This book should be used as a tool to help you change yourself and others. At the end of each chapter, you will find a "Reflection and Discussion" section with questions designed to stimulate contemplation and application. This section is divided into two parts, "Personal Steps to Change" and "Organizational Steps to Change." The personal questions are designed to help you grow. The organizational questions are designed to help you understand and alter the organization in which you work. I suggest that you keep a journal as you read this book. Read a chapter, and then write the answers to the questions in your journal.

The chapters in this book can be used as tools for change. Most of the chapters are very short and can stand alone. You may want to use them to influence the thinking of others. The organizational questions at the end of each chapter might be used as thinking tools for an individual, to hold discussions in a personal discussion group, to expand the awareness of a work group within your organization, or to teach in a classroom situation. Feel free to alter the questions to obtain the impact you desire.

Learning from Harvey

The ideas and experiences for this book have been inside me for a long time. Three times I tried unsuccessfully to write this book. Something wasn't right. Conveying the messages I felt so strongly about seemed difficult. I was internally blocked, and it took me quite a while to discover why.

The challenge I faced was how to communicate the relevance of initiating deep change within individuals or organizations. I wanted to help people develop the courage to step outside their old roles and to evaluate and establish new ones. However, I was unwilling to model the process for the reader. It was easier for me to remain a distant and analytical academic than to venture into new, unexplored territory. Consequently, each time I attempted to write this book, my efforts ground to a halt, and I couldn't understand why. Then I read Harvey Penick.

Penick was not a university scholar, but he was a great teacher. He spent his life teaching people how to swing a golf club. A few years ago, he wrote a short book, *Harvey Penick's Little Red Book*, that immediately became a best-seller. As I read his book, I knew he was a kindred spirit. He was a teacher whose job it was to improve the knowledge and performance of other people. Overall, he was a change agent who loved both what he was doing and the students who wanted to learn.

Yet there was something more. What was so special about Penick's book? Many professional teachers have written books about golf, but few of them ever become instant best-sellers. His book did not read like most golf self-help books. It was not a list of rules and procedures. It was actually his journal. Each time he had an important learning or teaching moment, a stimulating conversation, or an important insight, he recorded it in his journal. It contained rich, riveting stories that captured the imagination and interest of readers, tempted them to think differently, and motivated them to try new ideas. He loved golf, and by sharing his most cherished stories, he exposed himself to his audience. I know he built a relationship with me. He shared his passion and captured my attention.

Given Penick's example, I decided that to meet my objective, I needed to write from both my head and my heart. This book had to model what I was asking others to do. The idea was daunting, but I had to step out of my old role and try something new, to abandon my safe academic role for a time and risk the criticism of my university colleagues. Despite my initial discomfort, I persevered, and the blocked feeling soon disappeared.

As I reduced my own hypocrisy gap, my sense of integrity increased, as did my energy for this project. Drawing on my encounter with Penick's book, I wanted to write a book that interwove my poignant personal experiences as a change agent with my academic background. I wanted to write a book that would be both relevant and interesting and help us approach the ever-changing global environment with a sense of enlightenment and adventure.

This book is written with the hope that it will guide us as we strive to navigate deep change within ourselves or our organizations and that it will provide us with the strength to meet the many challenges we will face.

Acknowledgments

Every book owes a debt to a wide array of people. Given the nature of this book, the debt extends to nearly everyone I have ever known, worked with, or read. There are many stories in this book. They reflect numerous life experiences. To respect the privacy of the many people involved, I have kept all but the most known episodes anonymous. I have intentionally distorted some of the stories to ensure confidentiality. In doing so, I have nevertheless tried to retain the integrity of the original plot.

I would like to thank my professional colleagues at the two universities at which I have toiled over the past two decades, the State University of New York, Albany, and the University of Michigan. I am particularly grateful to the following people who have provided help on parts of various drafts: Ken Anbender, Susan Ashford, Vaughn Bryson, Kim Cameron, Kathy A. Clark, Corinne Coen, Gelaye Debebe, Jane Dutton, Rachel Ebert, Marty Edwards, Michael Jibson, Deb Meyerson, Rob Passick, Bob Robb, Gretchen

Spreitzer, Lynda St. Clair, Ellen Toronto, Karl Weick, Gil Whitaker, Joe White, and David Whetten.

I also want to thank the people who have invited me into their organizations and their lives.

Finally, I want to thank my wife, Delsa, an empowered and internally directed leader who faces deep change with courage and is gifted in helping others do the same. I appreciate her example.

Ann Arbor, Michigan   Robert E. Quinn
June 1996

The Author

Robert E. Quinn holds the M. E. Tracy Collegiate Professorship in the Organizational Behavior and Human Resource Management Group at the University of Michigan School of Business. He teaches in both the MBA and Executive Education Programs and is known for innovative instructional efforts.

Quinn is particularly interested in issues concerning leadership, vision, and change and has published numerous articles on these and related topics. His two most recent books are *Beyond Rational Management* and *Becoming a Master Manager*. Another book, *Diagnosing and Changing Organizational Culture* (with Kim S. Cameron), is due for publication by Jossey-Bass shortly after the present volume.

In addition to his research and writing experience, Quinn has been involved in the design and execution of a number of large-scale change projects.

Part I

Deep Change or Slow Death

1

Walking Naked into
the Land of Uncertainty

When most of us talk about change, we typically mean incremental change. Incremental change is usually the result of a rational analysis and planning process. There is a desired goal with a specific set of steps for reaching it. Incremental change is usually limited in scope and is often reversible. If the change does not work out, we can always return to the old way. Incremental change usually does not disrupt our past patterns—it is an extension of the past. Most important, during incremental change, we feel we are in control.

This book explores a much more difficult change process, the process of deep change. Deep change differs from incremental change in that it requires new ways of thinking and behaving. It is change that is major in scope, discontinuous with the past and generally irreversible. The deep change effort distorts existing patterns of action and involves taking risks. Deep change means surrendering control.

Most of us build our identity around our knowledge and competence in employing certain known techniques or abilities. Making a deep change involves abandoning both and "walking naked into the land of uncertainty." This is usually a terrifying choice, often involving a "dark night of the soul." It is therefore natural for each of us to deny that there is any need for a deep change. Fortunately, making a deep change is not something we need to do every day. In today's world of constant change, however, we need to do it more frequently than we have in the past.

Deep change can occur at both the organizational and the personal level. Insights into one level help us understand the other better. Here we will briefly examine the deep change process from the organizational level and then move to the personal level. Finally, we will consider the surprising relationship between the two.

Deep Change: The Organizational Perspective

A colleague once told me about a group of executives in a large state government who were interested in leadership training. They were particularly interested in teaching transformational leadership. They wanted to develop public administrators who would take initiative, who would make deep change in their organizations. Given the negative stereotype of public administrators as resistant bureaucrats, they wondered if there were any transformational leaders in any agency of their government. They decided to investigate and find out.

Their analysis revealed a number of cases of people who had made dramatic transformations within their various organizations. One person took over an office renowned for long lines and offended citizens. A year later, it was the best office in the system. Another person took over a hospital where conditions had long been scandalous. Two years later, it was a nationwide model. Eventually, they decided to make a video about some of these transformational leaders. Teams went out to interview the leaders. They returned with bad news. The video could not be made. In every single case, the transformational leader had, at least once, broken a state law. To transform the ineffective organization into an effective one, required forms were not turned in, regulations were ignored and directives were violated.

Does this mean that to be a transformational leader and make deep change in an organization, one has to break the law? No. It does always require, however, that someone must take some significant risks.

Organization and change are not complementary concepts. To organize is to systematize, to make behavior predictable. All organizations are based on systems of external and internal expectations. The external expectations may be informal, like the desire of a customer to buy a quality product at a reasonable price. Alternatively, the external expectations can actually be formalized into a law, requiring that an organization perform in certain ways. The internal expectations range from informal expectations to more formal routines, procedures, rules, or regulations. All these expectations help ensure predictable behavior.

The process of formalization initially makes the organization more efficient or effective. As time goes on, however, these routine patterns move the organization toward decay and stagnation. The organization loses alignment with the changing, external reality. As a result, customers go elsewhere for their products and services, and the organization loses its critical resources.

When internal and external alignment is lost, the organization faces a choice: either adapt or take the road to slow death. Usually the organization can be renewed, energized, or made effective only if some leader is willing to take some big risks by stepping outside the well-defined boundaries. When this happens, the organization is lured, pushed, or pulled into unknown territory. The resulting journey through the unknown is a terrifying experience, with the possibility of failure or death a reality rather than a metaphor.

At such times, organizational members face wicked problems, problems for which there are no existing answers. Facing imminent danger, they must "learn" their way, continually creating new possible solutions and inventive systems of organizing, systems that are aligned with today's, not yesterday's, external needs. If the new arrangements work, the organization usually experiences a period of great success. The outside world begins to deliver resources to the organization because the organization is creatively meeting the needs that exist in the present organizational environment.

It is now widely recognized that to remain competitive in today's global environment, organizations must frequently make deep change. What is not so widely recognized is that organizational members must also make deep change. Deep personal change is being demanded with more frequency today than in the past.

Deep Change: The Personal Perspective

Once I worked with senior executives at a highly successful organization in Asia. I was impressed with their efforts to design an organization that could make deep change more frequently and effectively. They told me that they were trying to become an "organic" organization. When I asked for a definition, they showed me a public document that stated that an organic organization is one that is "responsive, acts quickly and in a coordinated way, and can adjust and learn and grow." Many companies have similar statements. The next sentence, however, caught my attention. It read: "Only organic individuals can create an organic organization."

I was interested in this statement because so many organizations talk about becoming responsive, but few talk about the logical implication that naturally follows. Responsive organizations need responsive people. In an age of continuous change, organizations must match their environments by being more responsive, and people must match their organizations by being more responsive. If organizations must make deep change more frequently, so must the people who work in organizations.

Making deep change, however, is not easy. Organizations become structured and stagnant, and so do individuals. We have knowledge, values, assumptions, rules, and competencies that make us who we are. As the world around us changes, we lose our sense of alignment and begin to have problems. Often we can resolve these problems by making a small adjustment or an incremental change. Sometimes, however, we need to alter our fundamental assumptions, rules, or paradigms and develop new theories about ourselves and our surrounding environment. When this need emerges, we try to deny and resist it.

An Example of Deep Personal Change

I remember one executive with a large company that had never downsized. Suddenly, the company announced the need for such a reduction. This man was asked to inform a number of people, his close associates and friends, that they no longer had jobs. This painful task was barely completed when it was announced that another downsizing was necessary, and the process was repeated. This was followed by a third reduction. The psychological impact was overwhelming, and the surviving staff members were nearly immobilized.

This man described his own terror when he went home at night, looked at his children, and wondered what it would mean if he could not pay for their education or if he could not maintain his home. He wondered about his own market value. He had started out as an engineer, but now he was a manager—a specialist in the bureaucratic culture of his own particular company. In a world where many mid-level people were being eliminated, he feared he was useless. He felt betrayed and angry. He, like his colleagues, could now barely function at work. As a result, the company's performance fell, accelerating the entire vicious cycle.

After months of gut-wrenching agony, this man could take no more. He began to ask himself who he really was and what he really valued. He talked to his wife about these issues. Did he have an identity separate from the organization? Could they live on half his income if he switched jobs? He was surprised and delighted to discover that the answer to both questions was yes.

Answering these questions had a freeing effect. He felt personally empowered. He stopped worrying about the dangers of change and how he was seen by the organization. He began to ask himself what was needed in the present. He saw his immobilized colleagues and realized that he needed to do something to empower them. He designed a new role for himself. He carefully selected people and invited them into meetings and asked them what they wanted the company to look like in ten years. Initially they were startled by his question, but gradually they joined the process of designing the company's future. His sense of empowerment spread to others. Gradually, things began to improve.

In reflecting on the entire experience, the man told me he had an entirely new outlook on the concept of leadership. He talked about a paradox. He claimed that although he now acted much more independently, he cared more about the organization and was therefore twice as valuable.

This man had successfully negotiated the process of deep change. Because he was more internally driven, he was able to take part in the creation of his external world. He was no longer an externally determined response to his environment. He became both empowered and empowering. He was more capable of leading under conditions of continuous change. He was a more organic employee.

The Relationship Between the Two Levels

Facing an intense global economy, organizations and their members are having to reinvent themselves frequently. This is a top-down process. Pressure for change comes from the outside world, which forces the organization to reinvent itself. Organizational change then builds pressure for personal change. This sequence is assumed in nearly every discussion of organizational change strategy. The accuracy of this top-down model, however, blinds us to an equally accurate but seldom recognized model based on an opposing set of assumptions. It is a model of bottom-up change. It starts with an individual.

There is an important link between deep change at the personal level and deep change at the organizational level. To make deep personal change is to develop a new paradigm, a new self, one that is more effectively aligned with today's realities. This can occur only if we are willing to journey into unknown territory and confront the wicked problems we encounter. This journey does not follow the assumptions of rational planning. The objective may not be clear, and the path to it is not paved with familiar procedures. This tortuous journey requires that we leave our comfort zone and step outside our normal roles. In doing so, we learn the paradoxical lesson that we can change the world only by changing ourselves. This is not just a cute abstraction; it is an elusive key to effective performance in all aspects of life.

Scott Peck describes playing the role of psychotherapist in his book *The Road Less Traveled* (1978). Most of us do not readily identify with psychotherapists. Yet each of us needs to do what a psychotherapist tries to do—influence and change the behavior of others.

Like the rest of us, a psychotherapist learns to play a role. This begins with study and experience. Knowledge accumulates, assumptions are made, values formulate, competencies develop, and rules of operation are established. The psychotherapist, like a parent, teacher, salesperson, or executive, has a role and is deeply invested in that role. The role, however, may or may not fit the needs of a given client, child, student, customer, or organization. In fact, effectiveness—bringing change in another person—is dependent on change in the therapist. Carefully consider the following self-observation by Peck. It deserves several readings.

It has been said that the successful psychotherapist must bring to the psychotherapeutic relationship the same courage and the same sense of commitment as the patient. The therapist must also risk change. Of all the good and useful rules of psychotherapy that I have been taught, there are very few that I have not chosen to break at one time or another, not out of laziness and lack of discipline but rather in fear and trembling, because my patient's therapy seemed to require that, one way or another, I should step out of the safety of the prescribed analyst's role, be different and risk the unconventional. As I look back on every successful case I have had I can see that at some point or points in each case I had to lay myself on the line. The willingness of the therapist to suffer at such moments is perhaps the essence of therapy, and when perceived by the patient, as it usually is, it is always therapeutic. It is also through this willingness to extend themselves and suffer with and over their patients that therapists grow and change. Again as I look back on my successful cases, there is not one that did not result in some very meaningful, often radical, change in my attitudes and perspectives. It has to be this way. [p. 149]

The psychotherapist finds that deep change in the client necessitates the courage on the part of self to step outside the safety of traditionally prescribed roles. By exhibiting the courage to "walk naked into the land of uncertainty," the therapist models the way to improved health. The therapist does not instruct but "leads" the patient through the transformation. In making the terrifying journey, the therapist loses the old self and finds a new self, experiences greater meaning, and learns new perspectives. In changing self, the relationship is changed, and it becomes possible for the client to change also. The client has not only a model but also a system of meaningful support and challenge.

Here we find the surprising link between deep change at the personal level and deep change at the organizational level. The video mentioned earlier about the transformational leaders could not be made because the leaders took risks that were viewed as unacceptable. The state could not teach managers to break its own laws. Businesses have the same problem; they cannot teach people to deviate from their rules, policies, and procedures.

Excellence, however, never lies within the boxes drawn in the past. To be excellent, the leaders have to step outside the safety net of the company's regulations, just as the therapist had to step outside the safety of the traditionally defined role. To bring deep change, people have to "suffer" the risks. And to bring about deep change in others, people have to reinvent themselves.

Perhaps the most difficult thing to comprehend about deep change has to do with our relationships with others. When we see the need for deep change, we usually see it as something that needs to take place in someone else. In our roles of authority, such as parent, teacher, or boss, we are particularly quick to direct others to change. Such directives often fail, and we respond to the resistance by increasing our efforts. The power struggle that follows seldom results in change or brings about excellence. One of the most important insights about the need to bring about deep change in others has to do with where deep change actually starts.

It is true that in today's world, tumultuous conditions require organizations to make deep change more frequently. This in turn requires that individuals, too, make deep change more frequently. As observed before, it is a top-down process. Surprisingly, however, the opposite is also true: change can and does come from the bottom up.

Each of us has the potential to change the world. Because the price of change is so high, we seldom take on the challenge. Our fears blind us to the possibilities of excellence—and yet another formidable insight. This insight concerns the price of not making deep change. That price is the choice of slow death, a meaningless and frustrating experience enmeshed in fear, anger, and helplessness, while moving surely toward what is most feared.

Getting Lost with Confidence

Whereas most people flee from the thought of deep change, there are a few, like Scott Peck, who experience it often enough to reflect on it. They begin to see deep change as a developmental process that can be understood. Where others see only chaos, they see predictability. They understand that traditional learning is linked with the past—it is learning something that someone else already knows.

"Traveling naked into the land of uncertainty" allows for another kind of learning, a learning that helps us forget what we know and discover what we need. It leads to the discovery that helps us create the future. The few people who feel this way do so because of multiple past experiences in making the terrifying journey. After a while, terror turns to faith. These people "know how to get lost with confidence." That is, they know how to learn their way into the new and emerging world. They may be found at any level in an organization. They are master change agents capable of making deep change in themselves, in their relationships, and in their organization. They are internally driven leaders who understand the process of deep change.

REFLECTION AND DISCUSSION

➤ Personal Steps to Change

1. List the ten most significant personal changes you have ever made.

2. Sort the changes listed in Item 1 into two categories: incremental change and deep change.

3. Summarize your personal experience with deep change.

4. Provide an example of "walking naked into the land of uncertainty." Elaborate on what this phrase means to you.

5. Reread the quote from Scott Peck. Underline the key ideas, and describe your most important insights about bringing deep change in others.

6. What does it mean for someone to "get lost with confidence"?

7. Write your own definition of deep change.

➤ Organizational Steps to Change

1. List the ten most significant organizational changes you have ever witnessed.

2. Sort the changes in Item 1 into two categories: incremental change and deep change.

3. Summarize your personal experience with deep change in organizations.

4. In reflecting on the current functioning of your organization, review this chapter, and identify three insights that could make a difference today.

Confronting the Deep Change
or Slow Death Dilemma

Maintaining faith, courage, and energy in today's fiercely competitive world is not easy. Having to face the many challenges that occur in our lives and in our organizations and continually to resolve issues often corrodes our initiative and curtails our internal drive. Consider the following statements by executives at two different organizations:

I've been in this position for four years, and every year the work pressure has increased. My people are doing all they can just to hold on. I'm fifty-seven, and I'm doing all I can to hold on. I know we need to implement this thing. I just don't think we can do one more major change.

From a long-run perspective, there is no choice. But to tell you the truth, I'm not sure I have it in me. Of the eight vice-presidents, three are simply not up to taking this on. We're all around the same age, and we're all thinking, "If I can hang in just a couple of more years, this problem will belong to someone else." The issue is not what's good in the long run; it's how to survive right now.

These statements reflect the positions of many senior people who are buffeted by more demands than they can possibly meet. They are tired. Yet there is something more significant than personal burnout reflected in these statements. While both of these executives recognize that a deep change is needed in their organizations, both have opted to do nothing. They have chosen short-term personal survival over long-term collective responsibility.

These worn-down, disillusioned executives have made a conscious choice to let an unaddressed organizational problem fester and grow. The problem will eventually become a crisis, and many people will suffer. The practical implications of this deep change or slow death dilemma are illustrated by the following statements:

We chose slow death three years ago. The organization gave up a significant position in the industry because of an internal conflict between divisions with opposing philosophies. We needed real change, and everyone knew it. Yet no one was willing to engage it. The result was that we went from thirty-one thousand people to fewer than fifteen thousand in a two-year period. We are no longer a significant player, and there is no hope for the future. It is now just a matter of time.

Slow death is what we are about—a conservative, "don't rock the boat" culture; executives three to five years from retirement; little long-range planning; no vision; and denial of all external criticism. We make superficial changes in areas like technology and finance, but we make no real change in our basic structures and processes. We are on a course that is clear to all.

As a member of a top-management team, I experienced the slow death of a major corporation ten years ago. We had a conservative culture and resisted change until we were forced to engage an entire series of wild and uncoordinated changes. Finally, we went through a slow, painful death. It was a merger that few of our people survived. Now I'm experiencing it all over again. It is a haunting case of, "Hey, I've been here before."

We are dying. In the meantime, my boss goes around reducing everything to numbers and charts. He leaves the real task of leadership to others. Because we no longer believe in the organization's future, we're all tending to our own personal futures. I would love to be thinking about constructive alternatives, but it's simply too late.

I think our company has about twelve to eighteen months, and then it will be too late. To be truly competitive, we have to alter the underlying system. That means, however, getting past the ever-present and undeniably important daily tasks. It means doing more. I think we keep very busy because it's a kind of opium. We don't know how to confront the deep change process, so we keep ourselves busy with the normal stuff and try not to notice what's really happening. I'm not optimistic. There is no vision from the top, and the changes continue to be incremental. As I see it, we are very clearly choosing slow death.

Our top management people are ill-equipped to deal with the realities of our situation. We need sweeping changes. Their tools, obtained at the best business schools, are simply inadequate for facing our current competitive environment. They know how to manage, not how to lead. Besides, it's too late. We cannot be saved by willing it, even from the top. It's like trying to find a new golf swing the day before the Masters.

Slow Death: The Organizational Phenomenon

Slow death begins when someone, confronting the dilemma of having to make deep organizational change or accepting the status quo, rejects the option for the deep change. This decision results in the gradual (and occasionally not so gradual) disintegration of an organization, business, or industry.

The process of slow death has a number of common characteristics. Let us examine four of the most prominent.

Pervasiveness

The choice of slow death is not an isolated phenomenon. In today's global economy, it is verging on an epidemic, regularly occurring across a wide range of organizations. It is especially common in conservative, "don't rock the boat" cultures. But it is not confined to such organizations. Even in organizations experiencing great success (which can be another stimulant of stress and burnout), it is not unusual to find pockets of experienced, competent, and well-intentioned people who have opted for slow death. Change is needed, but this need is denied. The choice can be made anywhere, at any time, and at any level.

Violation of Trust

In choosing slow death, the decision makers may fully recognize the pressures for change. Instead of initiating the change, however, they choose to do other things. In this sense, the phenomenon of choosing slow death is not the same phenomenon as the often-told boiled frog story.

The boiled frog story is based on a laboratory experiment. A live frog is placed in a container of water that is gradually heated. Eventually the water boils, and the frog dies. In contrast, if a frog is taken from cold water and placed in a container of hot water, it immediately jumps out and thus manages to survive. Organizations are said to be like the frogs in the experiment. They are likely to be unconscious of slowly evolving changes.

The boiled frog metaphor does not capture an important aspect of the deep change or slow death phenomenon. When an executive admits that a change is needed but opts not to make it, the executive is making a conscious choice. The water is slowly heating up, and the executive knows that a leap to safety is possible, the strategic thought being, "If I can hang on just a couple of more years, this problem will belong to someone else." However, when the executive leaps to safety, the rest of the workforce is left with the problem. In this sense, the choice of slow death might be referred to as the "dead tadpole story." The frog leaps to safety, and the tadpoles are left to boil.

In this scenario, self-interest triumphs over collective responsibility. The selection of slow death has some moral overtones. It involves a violation of trust and responsibility, often leading to guilt. Because of the moral implications, the issue becomes undiscussable in the organization. Organizational members fake ignorance of the situation while fully understanding that their organization is in serious trouble. The impact of this problem is enormous.

Thirst for Vision

Executives often behave as if the problems they are having are a secret. However, that is seldom the case. People know when a critical issue is being ignored: "We needed real change. Everyone knew it, but no one was willing to engage it."

People slowly lose hope and begin to feel trapped by their circumstances. They often cope by withdrawing or, conversely, by staying busy with insignificant issues. "I think we keep very busy because it is a kind of opium." These people, like their superiors, become increasingly self-interested and begin to attend to their own futures. Experience suggests that they would love to consider constructive alternatives, and even at the darkest moment would do so, if given a reason. During troubled times, people thirst for effective leadership. They crave a vision that has credibility.

Providing such a vision, however, is a difficult task. Some executives find that it is much easier to generate numbers and spreadsheets than it is to provide visionary leadership. Disseminating one more rational analysis, however, may be like passing out canteens full of sand to people dying from thirst.

Burnout

Relative lack of energy is another issue. There are people who know how to lead, who understand deep change and the enormous investment of energy and resources that are necessary, yet they cannot bring themselves to initiate the process. There is no energy left. They are victims of burnout. So they continue to go through the motions, finding it difficult to discover interest and relevance in their work. What they need is deep change at the personal level, a reinvention of their professional role, a revolution in their priority list, a recognition that maintenance is production and that their "absolute musts" really "must" be delegated to someone else.

Few people are very good at reinventing themselves. They often choose the destructive alternative of staying very busy. It may not be effective behavior, but it has the effect of a good narcotic. It diverts attention from the real issue and temporarily saves them from having to tackle and resolve the actual problem.

Three Strategies for Confronting Slow Death at the Personal Level

Many of you will recognize the phenomenon being discussed. You may work in an organization that causes feelings of desperation. You may find yourself withdrawing. There are three strategies for confronting the problem of slow death.

Strategy 1: Peace and Pay

Walking down the hallway of a large government agency, I passed numerous offices and work areas. As people moved about, their body language suggested that what they were doing was not very urgent. My companion observed, "Here we house the legions of the walking dead." I have never forgotten that analogy because the imagery seemed to express something very real and at the same time something very sad about the people who work in such settings.

When people join the legions of the walking dead, they begin to live lives of "quiet desperation." They tend to experience feelings of meaninglessness, hopelessness, and impotence in their work roles, often taking on the role of "poor victim." A victim is a person who suffers a loss because of the actions of others. A victim tends to believe that salvation comes only from the actions of others. They have little choice but to whine and wait until something good happens. Living with someone who chooses to play the victim role is draining; working in an organization where many people have chosen the victim role is absolutely depressing. Like a disease, the condition tends to spread.

In today's organizations, many people are dying, not physically, but psychologically. To turn this situation around, for the healing process to begin, people must engage in deep personal change—change that will only occur when people take active charge of their own lives. This is a very uncomfortable concept for most people.

When someone makes the initial decision to avoid confronting a difficult situation, a negative process is triggered. The person becomes deeply frustrated and eventually quits trying. Often, without fully realizing it, the person has taken on the victim's role. Instead of initiating deep change, the person consciously chooses a destructive path that inexorably progresses toward slow death.

In recent years, this phenomenon has become more apparent. As organizations try to cope with external change, the level of stress in the workplace increases. As a result, people become frustrated and despondent, and their productivity decreases. Pessimism and despair permeate the atmosphere.

How does an individual cope in an organizational environment that is saturated with depression and discouragement? One strategy is very natural. Recently, the director of human resources at a large corporation articulated the strategy when she said, "Seventy-five percent of our middle managers have opted for peace and pay."

Peace and pay means "don't rock the boat," "maintain the status quo," "keep your head in a shell," "come in at eight and go home at five," "don't take any risks." Vast numbers of people choose exactly this behavioral strategy. When people do this, they are coping with slow death by choosing slow death.

Their resignation traps them in a vicious cycle from which escape is difficult. They shake their heads and condemn the organization, rightly noting that the organization is dying and wrongly assuming that they are not.

The peace-and-pay strategy is a form of mental illness. Actively choosing peace and pay means deliberately joining the legions of the walking dead. Making deep change in ourselves is not something we do for the organization; we do it for ourselves. It is a choice to be alive.

Strategy 2: Active Exit

When most middle managers are asked how to cope in a proactive way within an organization that is experiencing slow death, they present statements that can be reduced and integrated into the following four-step strategy:

- Follow a preventive medicine regimen and maintain a healthy lifestyle.

- Maintain a mental picture that accepts the probability of leaving.

- Stay in touch with the market and think creatively about alternative career paths.

- When it becomes most feasible, change jobs.

The *active exit* strategy is curious in that it is the most proactive process a reactive person can follow. There is some value in each of the four statements. They suggest the active management of stress, confronting reality, career management, and the courage to make a career change. When people actively pursue this strategy, they are exhibiting more self-responsible conduct than the passive choice of peace and pay.

There are, however, some problems with the active exit strategy. The various steps are primarily self-oriented. Individuals who choose this strategy are in effect contributing to slow death at the organizational level. The original problems are likely to get progressively worse for peers and subordinates. Furthermore, some people who choose this strategy make a painful discovery. They arrive at their new organization only to find that the new situation is very similar to the one they just left. In our world of hyperchange, most organizations are trying to resolve the same problems, with somewhat similar results. The grass is not always greener on the other side of the fence.

There is an interesting note about this strategy. When I present stories about senior managers who are choosing slow death for their organizations, middle managers become morally indignant. When, however, they are asked for an alternate approach to peace and pay, they construct the active exit strategy. I find little difference between the people who pursue the active exit strategy and the senior person who says, "In two more years, I'm out of here, and it will be someone else's problem." They are in fact both employing the same strategy. It is most difficult to see our own hypocrisy.

Strategy 3: Deep Change

One day, I explained the concept of slow death to Ellen Toronto, a practicing psychologist. She made an interesting comment:

> At the personal level, I deal with this issue every day. Every time a client comes to me with a problem, what I find is that the person is experiencing slow death. What I try to help such persons see is that they have a choice. They can continue to experience slow death, or they can make a deep change. Most do not have the courage to

engage the process of deep change, and so most are not cured. The challenge is to provide them with enough encouragement, help, and support that they dare to try.

Listening to this statement, I was struck by three points. The first had to do with the behavior she described. We go to see people like Ellen because we are desperate for help. We are experiencing slow death, and she helps us see that the pain we are experiencing is something we actively choose and that we can choose a more healthy alternative.

The second point is that we do not tend to choose the healthy alternative. We actually seem to prefer slow death. Slow death is the devil we know, so we prefer it to the devil we do not know. The alternative, being clarified by the therapist, may appear to be the road to fast death. It certainly involves self-modification and deep change. Deep change requires discipline, courage, and motivation. We would rather experience the pain of slow death than the threat of changing ourself.

The third point has to do with perspective. Previously, I had viewed slow death as an organizational issue, not as a personal issue for people working in organizations. I thought of slow death as something objective and far removed from me. Suddenly I realized that it was something much more basic. The tendency to choose slow death exists in everyone's life, including mine.

This was a very painful realization. I became fascinated by my own defense mechanisms, all the ways I could deny the fact that I was sometimes lazy or lacked courage. I became intrigued with the link between embracing disconfirming feedback, seeing and hearing unpleasant things about myself, and the process of growth. It wasn't long before I realized that if I was not continually growing, I was slowly dying.

One of my students left me the following statement:

Perhaps death is a much more constant companion than I realize. Organizational, professional, physical, and psychological death are similar in that they are hard to face. To choose death is to choose to cease to be. Such a choice is a horror to contemplate.

Perhaps in confronting the choice of slow death or deep change, I have come to understand that life is a constant process of deaths and rebirths. In understanding this, I am more free to grow and become more responsive to the individuals around me.

Over time, I began to understand that I needed to consider the reality of death more fully—and not just physical death but all forms of decay. It was important that I engage it, envision it, make it come alive, and see it for what it might be. Essentially, I needed to consider the various paths that lead to that envisioned state. Maybe with a living vision of death, the costs of taking more healthy paths would not appear so dear. Conceivably, upon reexamining my views on decay and ultimately death, I would have the discipline and courage to engage deep change.

In examining myself, I would find the capacity to live more fully and manage more effectively. In examining how managers and organizations cope with the problem of slow death, I was learning something very important about myself and about everyone else. I was learning that none of us can afford to avoid the confrontation of slow death. We all must choose the strategy of deep change.

➤ **Personal Steps to Change**

1. Identify several times in your life when you felt either overwhelmed or bored.

2. Identify a time that you felt like a victim. Specify your feelings and behavior.

3. Describe a time when you chose an active exit strategy and left an uncomfortable situation. What did you learn from the experience?

4. Identify a part of your life in which you feel like you are currently experiencing very little meaning.

5. Write a personal reaction to each of the following statements:

   In today's organizations many people are dying, not physically, but psychologically.

   Making deep change in ourselves is not something we do for the organization; it is something we do for ourselves. It is the choice to be alive.

   Perhaps in confronting the choice of slow death or deep change, I have come to understand that life is a constant process of deaths and rebirths. In understanding this, I become more free to grow and become more responsive to the individuals around me.

   I, like all other people, am guilty of choosing slow death. This is a very painful realization. I became fascinated by my own defense mechanisms, all the ways I could deny the fact that I was sometimes lazy or lacked courage. I became fascinated with the link between embracing disconfirming feedback, seeing and hearing unpleasant things about myself, and the process of growth.

➤ Organizational Steps to Change

1. It might be useful to stop and reflect on the kind of culture in which you work. Respond to the questions below by employing the following scale:

   1. Strongly disagree

   2. Disagree

   3. Neither agree nor disagree

   4. Agree

   5. Strongly agree

   In my organization:

   ____ The culture values conservative decisions.

   ____ Most change is incremental.

   ____ Deep change is avoided.

   ____ External criticism is explained away and ignored.

   ____ There is a short-term, day-to-day operating perspective.

   ____ Authority figures focus on management rather than leadership.

   ____ People have a sense of hopelessness.

   ____ There are needed changes that no one is willing to engage.

   ____ The failure to make needed change is undiscussable.

2. Having responded to the questions in Item 1, are you able to think of any ways or places in which your organization is experiencing slow death? Describe what is happening.

3. Considering your answers to the question in Item 2, list some action steps that should be taken to make things better.

Part II

Personal Change

3

The Fear of Change

I once worked with a top management team of a very large company. I came to know the individuals very well. They were bright, honest, sincere, and hardworking. In an effort to improve their organization, they had decided to send all the senior people to a well-known seminar on quality. These executives, upon returning from the enlightening seminar, decided to implement the ideas in their organization. Together they developed a reasonable plan and initiated the change effort.

A short time later, while we were doing some strategic planning, the team made numerous references to the new quality philosophy. They were making assumptions that quality, morale, productivity, and profit would all improve because of the new philosophy. They listed the alterations in behavior and productivity they expected to see in each area of the company. They were planning the future of their company around the premise that these significant changes would happen.

Upon hearing their comments, I shared with them a story that was told to me by a vice-president at another company. Three years before, that company had sent all its senior executives to the same seminar. They also anticipated that their new plan would yield dramatic improvements in quality, morale, productivity, and profit. However, three years later, they found that their immense effort had little, if any, impact.

Given the sizable investment they had already made, the executives were transfixed by my story. They waited anxiously for an explanation of the failure. Almost in unison they asked, "Why did it fail?" Instead of explaining, I asked them to tell me why it failed.

A long, heavy silence fell in the room. Finally, one of the most influential members of the group said, "The leaders of the company didn't change their behavior." I nodded and pointed out that they themselves had made a lot of assumptions about the behavior that was going to change in others. Now I challenged them: "Identify one time when one of you said that you were going to change your behavior."

Again there was a long pause. Something important and unusual was happening. The members of this group were suddenly seeing something that few people ever clearly see—the incongruity of asking for change in others while failing to exhibit the same level of commitment in themselves.

Since they expressed a sincere desire to change their organization, they asked me for advice. I described some simple practices that had succeeded for others. These practices would give them the tools they needed to change their stagnant patterns and systems. They were quiet for a time—a time of quiet terror and inner reflection. It was as if they were standing at the edge of a very dangerous cliff and peeking over. They decided to adjourn and think about the issues.

It is tempting to belittle these people. How dare they exhibit such arrogance? Though we may be tempted to condemn these managers, we should first reflect on what we would do in similar situations. We regularly exhibit the same behavior. In confronting life's problems, we readily see the shortcomings of others and how these shortcomings contribute to the problem at hand. The problem is always caused by the boss, peer, subordinate, spouse, child, schoolteacher, or some other person.

We cannot easily recognize that the problem is part of the system in which we play an active role. Our first inclination is always from a perspective that externalizes the problem, keeps it somewhere "out there." Because the problem is out there, it is always others who need to change. Our first thought is to tell them to change. Our second is to force them. Painful experience tells us that this route is usually less than successful and often disastrous, producing undesirable and unproductive results.

Telling, Coercing, and the Checklist Mentality

Years ago, I developed a simple role play. In this role play, two volunteers are asked to come forward. They are given a brief description of their roles. They are spouses who experienced a whirlwind courtship and have just returned from their honeymoon. After a wonderful breakfast, the wife leans back and lights up a cigarette. Since meeting his wife, the man has had but one reservation, her smoking. He decides that he can no longer suppress his concern.

At this point, I ask the husband to begin a conversation with his beloved. The dynamics are very predictable. The husband tells the wife that her smoking is a problem. She grows defensive and angry. He resorts to factual information and reports that there is a scientific link between smoking and cancer. She rebuffs this argument. Then he brings up the issue of commitment and intimate relationships, in some way suggesting that their marriage may not survive. She usually agrees.

Life is full of situations in which we would very much like another person to change behavior. We want our neighbors to not impinge on our rights. We want our child to not leave the bike in the middle of the driveway. We want our mother to stop interfering. We want people who work for us to have more of a sense of urgency.

In our attempts to address such problem situations, we usually begin by simply telling these persons what the problem is and how they might change. When the change is small or clearly to their liking, this strategy tends to work. In most cases, however, it fails. The other persons have little interest in responding to our need. If the issue at hand really matters, we then turn to coercion, often suggesting or making some kind of threat. Like a criminal with a pointed gun, we can get, for a short while, the behavior change we desire, but it is unlikely to last, and the long-term relationship tends to be damaged.

In organizations, I watch managers engage in the strategy of change by telling. The manager knows that the people in the organization should make some important change, so this item goes on their "to do" list. At the appropriate time, the manager gives a speech or writes a memo instructing people to change. The manager then places a check next to the item on the "to do" list. The change has been implemented. What more can be expected?

Weeks or months later, signals begin to emerge suggesting that the requested change has not taken place. Usually the manager chooses to ignore these signals. Sometimes, however, the pressure for the change is too high and the problem cannot be neglected. Next the manager will usually resort to coercion. This results in short-term compliance and long-term resistance. The common result is for the change effort to fail.

It is striking to me that so many new programs that initiate change in organizations fail. It is also striking that once a change effort fails, the effort tends to be ignored. These failures are seldom analyzed. Such analysis would be too painful. As a result, little learning takes place.

When we experience failure, it is natural to externalize the problem—to blame some factor that was outside our control. Once in a while this actually does happen. But I have seldom heard anyone say, "The change didn't happen because I failed to model the change process for everyone. I failed to reinvent myself. It was a failure of courage on my part."

One key to successful leadership is continuous personal change. Personal change is a reflection of our inner growth and empowerment. Empowered leaders are the only ones who can induce real change. They can forcefully communicate at a level beyond telling. By having the courage to change themselves, they model the behavior they are asking of others. Clearly understood by almost everyone, this message, based in integrity, is incredibly powerful. It builds trust and credibility and helps others confront the risk of empowering themselves.

At the personal level, the key to successful living is continuous personal change. Personal change is the way to avoid slow death. When we are continually growing, we have an internal sense of meaning and impact. We are full of energy and radiate a successful demeanor. To have such feelings in a continually changing environment, we must continually realign ourselves with our environment. This requires that we do an unnatural thing—that we exercise the discipline to take an unusual perspective.

Taking the Third Perspective First

A friend of mine, Michael Jibson, tells a story about taking his family to the San Francisco Zoo. Soon after arriving at the zoo, the family walked into a playground area. Michael's smallest son dearly loved playgrounds, particularly the swings. The boy quickly raced over, jumped into a swing, and began pumping himself skyward.

After a short time, the other children were ready to move on. The youngest, however, was still happily swinging. The siblings tried to persuade him to leave but were unsuccessful. The boy's mother tried a more caring approach, but she, too, failed miserably. The other children then began to complain loudly. A drama was emerging, and strangers were stopping to watch. Michael's wife looked at him, her unspoken message clear: "You are the father of this child. Do something!"

Michael, having been to the zoo before, knew that around the corner was a carousel. He also knew that the boy loved carousals even more than he loved the swings. So Michael explained that there was a carousel around the corner and that the youngster would be even happier there.

Nearly any experienced parent can predict what happened next. The boy was unmoved by the fatherly logic. Michael's frustration peaked, and persuasion turned to threat. Finally, the boy was dragged, kicking and squealing, from the swing and continued to protest until the family arrived at the carousel. Suddenly his eyes grew large with excitement. His tears disappeared as he mounted a wooden horse and smiled and waved to his parents.

We can reflect on this story from at least three perspectives. First, we can take the uninvolved perspective of the passing stranger. We can shake our heads in judgment of the parents who failed to perform their roles without resorting to force. The perspective is that of the distant, analytical observer, of the uninvolved judge, of the Monday morning quarterback. In our own lives, we slip into this perspective easily and often.

Second, we could take the perspective of the two loving but frustrated parents who were struggling to make an intervention in a real situation. The perspective of the responsible actor, trying to make change in the world, is a challenge for the ages. At the conceptual and emotional levels, we often aspire to it. From the perspective of observed actor, we often consciously or unconsciously flee from it. Here we often, like the parents in the story, experience frustration and failure.

Finally, there is the perspective of the self-centered little boy holding tightly to his swing. Our first temptation is to argue that for mature adults such as ourselves, that is too big a stretch and hardly worth consideration. This is, of course, a rationalization to protect us from considering the most painful perspective of all: one of the last things we want to consider is our own selfishness and immaturity. We resist reflecting on our own fear of change. Yet the truth is that we are exactly like the immature and selfish boy who refuses to leave the swing.

The problem is that to grow, to take the journeys on which our growth is predicated, we must confront our own immaturity, selfishness, and lack of courage. In a sense, life is all about our forceful, often overpowering need to take journeys, yet our tendency is to grip the swings ever more tightly. The decisions we make about our journeys determine how our self is aligned with our surrounding environment.

➤ Personal Steps to Change

1. Select and describe a recent situation in which you tried to get someone to make an important change in behavior.

2. The two most frequent strategies for changing others are telling and coercing. In your situation in Item 1, were these two strategies present? How did they contribute to the final outcome?

3. In trying to change others, it is very difficult to see ourselves as a part of the problem. Reflecting on your situation in Item 1, imagine how you might have been a contributor to the problem pattern. How might you have changed the pattern by changing yourself?

4. Write your personal reaction to the following: "The problem is that to grow, to take the journeys on which our growth is predicated, we must confront our own immaturity, selfishness, and lack of courage. In a sense, life is all about our forceful, often overpowering need to take journeys, yet our tendency is to grip the swings ever more tightly. The decisions we make about our journeys determine how our self is aligned with our surrounding environment."

➤ Organizational Steps to Change

1. The first story in this chapter concerns a group of managers attempting to improve quality in their organization. They assume that many changes are necessary in the organization, but they never think about changing their own behavior. It is suggested that when leaders fail to change themselves, the organization does not change. Think about an occasion when someone has done this in your organization. Describe the process and the results.

2. How often have you seen a leader model new behaviors that would initiate a desired organizational change? Select a particular example, and specify what you learned from observing the example.

3. Think of a current change effort in your organization that is in the telling, coercing, or forcing stage. What do you predict will happen next?

4. What might be done to improve the effectiveness of the change effort described in Item 3?

4

The Heroic Journey

Energy is neither created nor destroyed. At any given moment, it flows toward some points in the universe and away from others. The amount of energy we feel has much to do with the alignment between ourself and our surrounding environment. We can be aligned with our environment in such a way that we feel either strong and empowered or weak and powerless.

When we feel the strongest and at the "top of our game," we radiate large amounts of energy. When this energy and drive are directed toward some important task, good things tend to happen. As we experience success, we learn and grow. We gain a new perspective. As we apply this new understanding, we tend to become even more energized. During these periods, the self and the surrounding environment are more in alignment.

A key insight about dynamic alignment can be derived from an observation made by Fred Kofman and Peter Senge (1993). They point out that the self is a form of energy, and its state is entirely dependent on its relationship with the surrounding environment. They state:

> Newtonian physicists were startled to discover that at
> the core of the atom, at the center of matter there is . . .
> nothing, no thing, pure energy. When they reached

into the most fundamental building block of nature, they found a pregnant void—stable patterns of probability striving to connect with other patterns of probability. This discovery revolutionized the physical sciences, initiating the quantum era.

By the same token, we are startled to discover that at the core of the person, at the center of selfhood there is . . . nothing, pure energy. When we reach into the most fundamental basis of our being we find a pregnant void, a web of relationships. When somebody asks us to talk about ourselves, we talk about family, work, academic background, sports affiliations, etc. In all this talk, where is our "self"? The answer is nowhere, because the self is not a thing, but as Jerome Brunner says, "a point of view that unifies the flow of experience into a coherent narrative"—a narrative striving to connect with other narratives and become richer. [p. 14]

What does this mean? These statements imply that the self is not a thing but an unfolding process. We are energized when we are learning and progressing, and we begin psychologically to die when we allow ourselves to stagnate. That is where we encounter the process of slow death.

Relationships often play a key role. We have our greatest sense of joy and meaning when we connect with others in mutually enhancing ways. When we are disempowered, when we choose "peace and pay," we do not create or attract mutually enhancing relationships. We are left to ourselves, depleted, tired, and disempowered.

If decay begins when we choose to stop growing, why do we ever stop? The answer is that there are times when we cannot "unify the flow of experience into a coherent narrative." These are the times when we lose our sense of self and our inaction causes us to stagnate. Like the resistant boy on the playground, we are tightly gripping our swing and cannot let go. Our internal voice tells us to do something, to move on, to engage the unknown, but our courage fails. We remind ourselves how much we value the pleasure we derive from the swing, and we tighten our grip.

The swing might represent any pattern of old and comfortable behavior—a job, a habit, a relationship, or any other pattern. The present self is very tied to this established pattern. We sense that without the pattern, the self would no longer exist.

This view exacerbates our problem. The longer we stay on the swing, the less courage we have to change. We get caught in a vicious cycle and can see no way out. At such times, the notion of realignment seems utopian at best. We come to believe that we are powerless, reflecting that all human beings are determined by their environments—that there is no such thing as individuality, freedom, choice, or impact. We are so into this sense of defeated and frustrated self that we do not recognize that our best self is not the old self but a new self that is slowly emerging.

A Framework for Personal Change: The Hero's Journey

In today's changing global economy, uncertainty and constant change are an ongoing concern and an ever-present reality. Under these conditions, we often feel insecure, and we grasp for any source of stability and predictability.

In the workplace, we particularly yearn for a sense of direction. Working with large organizations, I often encounter middle managers who express a need to know the "vision"—the general framework of future direction that will guide and unite their efforts, a unifying vision that will allow them to make informed decisions within their own zone of discretion. They yearn for a leader who can align the internal and external realities and make the organization successful. They want someone who can guide them through the uncharted, threatening world of the unfamiliar. They long to feel confident that their organization, of which they are an integral part, will strive to be a vital and healthy concern.

Most of us have very high expectations of our leaders, and we are easily and quickly disillusioned by their failure to meet our expectations. We seldom, however, hold the same expectations for ourselves. We feel little responsibility to be the person who empowers self and, in so doing, empowers the surrounding community. Contemplating this tendency of ours, I am reminded of the work of Joseph Campbell, the well-known mythologist. He provides some interesting insights into the process of energizing self and community.

Common usage defines the word *myth* to mean something untrue. There is another use for the word, however. A myth is also a story that provides meaning and insight. It helps us make sense of our world and our existence in it. It may be a fictional story, like the tale of Cinderella, or a true story, like that of George Washington crossing the Delaware River. In either case, the myth or story provides a psychological framework, a schema or paradigm that can guide decisions.

Some myths, in their underlying message, are common across many cultures. Such myths are believed to reflect some basic needs in the human psyche. Campbell (1949) has identified a common myth that occurs in every culture. He calls it the hero's journey. The myth is about personal enlightenment and collective renewal. Campbell describes the hero's journey as follows:

> The mythological hero, setting forth from his common day hut or castle, is lured, carried away, or else voluntarily proceeds to the threshold of adventure. There he encounters a shadow presence that guards the passage. The hero may defeat or conciliate this power and go alive into the kingdom of the dark (brother-battle, dragon-battle, offering, charm), or be slain by the opponent and descend in death (dismemberment, crucifix-

ion). Beyond the threshold, then, the hero journeys through a world of unfamiliar yet strangely intimate forces, some of which severely threaten him (test), some of which give magical aid (helpers). When he arrives at the nadir of the mythological round, he undergoes a supreme ordeal and gains his reward. The triumph may be represented as the hero's sexual union with the goddess-mother of the world (sacred marriage), his recognition by the father-creator (father atonement), his own divinization (apotheosis), or again—if the powers have remained unfriendly to him—his theft of the boon he came to gain (bride-theft, fire-theft); intrinsically it is an expansion of consciousness and therewith of being (illumination, transfiguration, freedom). The final work is that of the return. If the powers have blessed the hero, he now sets forth under their protection (emissary); if not, he flees and is pursued (transformation flight, obstacle flight). At the return threshold the transcendental powers must remain behind; the hero reemerges from the kingdom of dread (return, resurrection). The boon that he brings restores the world (elixir). [p. 245]

The hero's journey is a story of individual transformation, a change of identity. In embarking on the journey, we must leave the world of certainty. We must courageously journey to a strange place where there are a lot of risks and much is at stake, a place where there are new problems that require us to think in new ways.

Because there is much at stake, we must engage and resolve the problems before us. To do this successfully, we must surrender our present self—we must step outside our old paradigms. This venture outside of our current self will cause us to think differently. To continue our journey is to reinvent the self. It is then that our paradigms change and we experience an "expansion of consciousness." We begin to realign ourself with our surrounding environment.

Not only do we view the world differently, but we view it more effectively.

Our new way of viewing the world also causes us to see ourselves differently. There is a change in our state of being, a change in self. As a result of this realignment of self, we can more effectively impact our environment. Success begins to breed success, and we are filled with drive and energy. In this way, we can empower others, and we become an asset to ourselves, our organizations, and our community.

Basically, the hero's journey is a theory of change. In some form, it exists in every culture. It is a theory of change that we all, at some level, understand. Yet the word *hero* can be problematic. There are many famous heroes. These people tend to appear almost larger than life. In taking the hero's journey, they do the seemingly impossible. Surviving their amazing feats, they gain our respect, and we confer on them near-deity status.

I like to think about the hero's journey in other terms. I like to think about a little boy who is being encouraged to leave a safe, known, and desirable place to journey to a place that he has only been told about. I like to think of the blue-collar laborer who, after an agonizing deliberation, decides to risk the job rather than follow an unethical directive. I like to think about the hero's journey in terms of you and me and our continual search for meaning and direction in our lives.

In our search for meaning and direction, we have a problem. Traditionally, our paradigms, myths, or scripts have told us what to do. They have helped organize our lives. Whenever we follow them, we feel safe. But today, our environment keeps changing. Because environments are dynamic and our myths are based in the past, our strategies often fail, and we feel a sense of alienation. Increasingly, it is becoming necessary for us to re-create our paradigms, myths, scripts, or frameworks.

New paradigms are created by engaging a new action path, one in which we must separate from the status quo and courageously face and tackle uncertainty. When successful, this process alters our original frameworks and our original self. We become highly aligned, successful, empowered, and able to help and inspire others. Only when this realignment is successful are we able to become leaders and change agents.

The problem is that the new alignment lies on the other side of uncertainty. In the next few chapters, I will describe some guidelines that can be employed by individuals interested in taking this journey.

REFLECTION AND DISCUSSION

➤ Personal Steps to Change

1. Provide an explanation of the following statement: "The self is not a thing but an unfolding process. We are energized when we are learning and progressing, and we begin psychologically to die when we allow ourselves to stagnate."

2. "When we are disempowered, when we choose 'peace and pay,' we do not create or attract mutually enhancing relationships. We are left to ourselves, depleted, tired, and disempowered." Make a list of the relationships in your life that are "mutually enhancing," that give you high levels of energy and drive and a deep sense of meaning.

3. Reread the description of the hero's journey. What experiences in your life might fit the description of the hero's journey? Make a list. Compare and contrast the experiences on your list. In doing the analysis, what insights emerge?

4. What would help you to take the hero's journey more frequently? How would your taking the "hero's journey" affect the relationships in your life?

➤ Organizational Steps to Change

1. Think about the hero's journey at the collective level. Have you ever seen a group, unit, or organization go on the hero's journey? Describe the process and its outcome.

2. Based on your organizational experience, explain the following statement: "Empowered leaders are the only ones who can induce real change. They can forcefully communicate at a level beyond

telling. By having the courage to change themselves, they model the behavior they are asking of others. Clearly understood by almost everyone, this message, based in integrity, is incredibly powerful. It builds trust and credibility and helps others confront the risk of empowering self."

3. Given the description of leadership in Item 2, who are the people in your organization who know how to lead?

4. In your organization, is there a need for leaders? If so, how would you use the framework of the "hero's journey" to accelerate the development of these leaders?

5

Finding Vitality

Some years ago, I was invited to a meeting of senior officers at one of the military academies. The officer in charge talked at length about the moral decay in society. There seemed to be no focus to his discussion, and I could not figure out what problem was actually concerning these men. Eventually it was revealed that some of the students at the academy were cheating on their exams. The cadets were not following the academy's honor system. The officers' explanation for the cadets' behavior was corruption in society. They felt that by the time an eighteen-year-old arrived at the academy it was too late; the cadet was irredeemable.

After a long discussion about the corruption in society, I attempted to turn the topic around. I asked if anyone in the room had served in Vietnam. Most had. I asked if any of them had participated in the phenomenon known as the body count. (This was a measurement system used to determine how American forces were performing in the war. At the end of each battle, the number of enemy dead were counted, and the number was reported. As this process unfolded, vastly exaggerated numbers were routinely reported.)

From the atmosphere of discomfort in the room, it was clear that some had participated. Why, I asked, would an *officer and a gentleman* (as opposed to an uncommissioned cadet) engage in such behavior? Answering my own question, I suggested that when an impossible objective is given to people in a large hierarchy and when it is accompanied by immense pressure to produce, the people in the organization will also experience growing pressure to engage in unethical behavior. An invisible form of corruption at the top, the exercise of authority without concern or demand without support, results in a very visible form of corruption at the bottom.

I then suggested that perhaps the problem with the cadets did not take root "out there" in society. Maybe large numbers of students were cheating because the system demanded and taught them to cheat. Were the arrangement of classes, the design of assignments and workloads, and traditional military values like "cooperate and graduate" combining to teach, require, and reward cheating? Was the problem in the cadets alone, or was it in the relationship between the cadets and the authority figures who were condemning and externalizing the problem?

There was a long silence. Finally, the man in charge spoke. He turned to the man next to him and, as if I had never said a word, resumed the old discussion about the moral decay in society. For the rest of the day they ignored me—I simply did not exist.

The behavior of these men was not surprising. They were practicing denial. Denial occurs when we are presented with painful information about ourselves, information that suggests that we need to make a deep change. Denial is one of several clear paths toward slow death. When we practice denial, we work on the wrong solutions or on no solutions at all. The problem grows worse as we become discouraged, and our vitality level declines.

Monitoring the Vitality Level

Bill was hired as a senior executive by a fast-growing company. He was excited about his new job but was troubled by the fact that a few members of the hiring committee believed that he did not have the requisite abilities. Wanting to show these people that he was the right man for the job, he made a commitment to work harder than he had ever worked in his life. His commitment paid off. Within a short time, everyone agreed that Bill was the right choice.

Over the next several years, Bill noted that the harder he worked, the more success he had. His mounting success reinforced his efforts. Then one day, his wife expressed some serious concern about his lifestyle. He was leaving for work at 4 A.M. and not returning home until late at night. She was unhappy about having to shoulder all the household responsibilities, and she was also anxious about the impact of his work schedule on his physical health. Bill patiently listened but made little change. When confronted a second time by his wife, Bill promised not to leave for work until after breakfast and to be home in time for dinner. He kept the promises, but his wife was not impressed. Bill was working out of his briefcase from 4 A.M. until breakfast and from the end of dinner until it was time for bed. Interestingly, the complaints did not come only from his wife. Bill noticed that his coworkers were also sending him subtle signals of displeasure.

Bill eventually decided to attend a retreat that was held on the West Coast. At one point, the participants were taken to the beach, where they were given crayons and some paper and asked to draw a picture of something on the beach. Bill walked until he was far away from the beach and well up into the sand dunes. Gazing slowly around, he sat down in front of a withered and dying old pine tree and drew the tree.

On the last day of the retreat, the participants were taken to a craft room and asked to create an object that represented the week. Bill thought the exercise was silly. Halfheartedly, he picked up a small log with a split in it. Then he selected a piece of tumbleweed and stuck it in the split in the log. He held up this creation for all to see and caustically said, "Here is my week."

As he looked at the object, he was awestruck by how much the tumbleweed resembled the dying pine tree. He was then overwhelmed by a powerful insight. He recalls, "I suddenly realized that

I was that dying old pine tree and that I was denying my need for nourishment of the self."

In taking a new job, Bill embarked on a new, challenging, and risky adventure—he was on the hero's journey. As he attacked his new job, he grew and developed. There was the feedback loop between his efforts and his energy level. The more he worked, the more successful he became. The renewed success brought him meaning and increased vitality and drive. He was in a self-reinforcing, virtuous cycle.

At some point, however, Bill crossed an invisible line, and his efforts began to bring diminishing returns. The virtuous cycle inverted. It became a self-reinforcing vicious cycle. The harder he worked, the less effective his efforts became, and this caused him to work harder, thus becoming even less effective.

Many of us have experienced a situation where we have crossed the invisible line and watched as our performance fell off, resulting in frustration and an increase in stress. The usual reaction is to work harder. Interestingly, psychologists believe that as the level of stress increases, the attention span diminishes.

People seek solutions to new problems in the same places where they found the old ones. In the face of stress and pressure, when the attention span diminishes, there is a tendency to become rigid. Instead of responding creatively, when innovative action is most needed, people increase their commitment to their old patterns. They implement their most ingrained natural response.

Karl Weick tells the story of a plane that is flown by U.S. pilots in North America and in Europe. Although the plane is essentially the same in both places, the ejection systems vary by location. In Europe, the pilot ejects through the bottom of the plane. In North America, the pilot ejects through the top of the plane. When pilots get in trouble in Europe, they are trained, as their last act, to roll the plane and eject themselves upward so they may parachute safely to earth. When they are transferred from Europe to the United States, they are retrained to use the procedure of simply ejecting themselves upward. An interesting problem occurs. In crisis, some of the transferred pilots, as their last act, turn their planes upside down and eject themselves to their death. Under stress they behave according to the most deeply held framework.

Most of us are like the people in these three stories. Warning signals that suggest a need for change tend to be denied. As performance levels fall, stress goes up, and vitality and drive wane. Our focus narrows, and we increase our commitment to our existing strategies, leading us toward greater difficulty.

To avoid the journey toward slow death, one of the most useful things we can do is monitor our level of vitality. We need to watch carefully for signs that we have crossed the invisible line. When this occurs, we need to think about breaking the logic of task pursuit and charting a course toward deep change and renewed vitality.

REFLECTION AND DISCUSSION

➤ **Personal Steps to Change**

1. Analyze the story about Bill, the hardworking executive, by answering the following questions:

   Why did he ignore the initial concerns expressed by his wife?

   Eventually he promised to change but could not. Why was the change so difficult?

   What did he have to do to come to the key insight that allowed him to finally change?

   What does it mean to deny "the need for nourishment of the self"?

2. Think of an episode in your life that is similar to Bill's experience. In your chosen episode, trace the evolution from the sense of challenge to the exhilaration of success to the loss of alignment. In what ways is your episode the same as Bill's? In what ways is it different?

3. When things are going well in your life, what are some of the indicators of high vitality?

4. How do you know when you have crossed the "invisible line" and your increasing efforts are bringing diminishing returns? How do you normally cope with the problem?

5. What steps can you take to ensure that you are assessing your own level of vitality accurately?

➤ Organizational Steps to Change

1. In the story about the military academy, why did the senior officer react as he did? How often in your organization do you see this same reaction?

2. The story of Bill could also apply to a group or an organization. When do groups or organizations exhibit high vitality? What are the indicators of high vitality?

3. Think of a time when you have observed a group progress from challenge to exhilaration to loss of alignment. Did the group practice denial? How?

4. Given your response to Item 3, what might be needed by such a group, and how could such a group be helped?

5. How would a group or unit examine its own level of vitality?

6

Breaking the Logic of Task Pursuit

In pursuing a task, we naturally follow our existing paradigms, scripts, or frameworks. These maps are the key to our past success. The problem is that as we experience success, we change, and so does the world. A map we have used in the past might be of limited value in new territory. In a new situation, if we cling to our old map, we might become deeply frustrated. At such times, we often become trapped in the *logic of task pursuit*.

The logic of task pursuit is best illustrated by a management parable that has been around for several decades. A hermit, who lived far out in a forest, would cut enough wood each summer to heat his cabin through the winter. One fall day, he heard on his shortwave radio that an early winter storm was heading for his area. Because he had not yet cut enough wood, he rushed to his wood pile.

Examining his dull and rusty saw, he realized that it needed sharpening. He paused for a moment, looked at his watch, looked at the height of his uncut wood pile, and shook his head. Instead of sharpening his saw, he began to cut. As he worked, he noted that the saw was getting increasingly dull and that he was working harder and harder. He told himself repeatedly that he needed to stop and sharpen the saw, but he continued to cut anyway. At the end of the day, as the snow began to fall, he sat exhausted next to a sizable pile of uncut wood.

This man was not ignorant. He knew his saw desperately needed sharpening. He also knew that the more he cut, the duller the blade would become. Yet he could not bring himself to stop and sharpen the saw. This man was a victim of the logic of task pursuit.

For most of us, under pressure, the pursuit of task drives out any thought of maintenance. Doing the right thing is driven out by the need to be busy. I refer to it as the "tyranny of the in-basket." We have too much to do to take the time necessary to do it right. Our individual drive toward task completion thwarts the need for routine maintenance.

The parable of the hermit is useful for helping us recognize that we have a blind spot that hinders our thinking. This parable, however, also has another level of application.

An organization is a collective entity for accomplishing specific tasks. Every organization has a group of systems—a cultural system, a strategic system, a technical system, and a political system. In an environment of constant change, each of these systems—like the hermit's saw—tends to wear down. Alignment within and between the systems is lost. We find ourselves working harder than ever, yet we benefit less and less from our efforts. As tension mounts, we look for someone to blame. The real problem, however, is embedded in the underlying organizational systems that have shifted out of alignment—with each other and sometimes with the external environment.

When an organization discovers that its systems need realignment, I am often asked to make a diagnosis. Senior executives seldom argue with my diagnosis, but they almost always argue with my recommendations. I am told, "What you don't understand is that we don't have the time to make the deep change you are recommending." This statement is accurate. There is no time. In coming to such a conclusion, the executive is choosing task over maintenance. The executive is also, however, choosing a future crisis. Sooner or later a crisis will occur and a price will be paid.

Breaking the Logic of Task Pursuit

How can we break the logic of task pursuit? To illustrate and answer this question, consider the story "The Day at the Beach" (1960) by Arthur Gordon. It was introduced to me and thousands of other undergraduates by a wonderful professor, Reed Bradford. It had a great impact on my life.

The story features a man experiencing deep frustration with his work. Each day, his sense of meaninglessness increases, and he can barely force himself to go to work in the morning. When he can stand it no longer, he goes to a doctor. The doctor listens to his complaints and then asks him where he was happiest as a child. The man responds that he had been happiest at the beach.

The doctor writes four directives or "prescriptions" on each of four slips of paper. The man is instructed to go to a beach the next day. He is to arrive before nine. He is to talk to no one, bring no reading material, and follow the directions on the slips of paper at nine, twelve, three, and six o'clock.

The man arrives at the beach well before nine o'clock but is extremely cynical. He is frustrated by the fact that there is no task to complete, no problem he can throw himself into solving. The time passes slowly.

At nine o'clock, he takes out the first slip and reads, "Listen carefully." The man concludes that the doctor must be mad. There is nothing to hear. He begins walking and notices that there are a variety of sounds emanating from the surf, sand, and other natural sources. He is attracted by these sounds and soon finds himself in deep contemplation. He is thinking about other things bigger than himself. He is comforted by this but still feels he should be engaged in a more productive task.

Noon arrives, and he reads the next slip: "Try reaching back." Back to what? he wonders. As he continues along the beach, he finds himself resurrecting memories of his past relationships. He remembers a fishing expedition with his deceased brother. He relives other family experiences, again feeling the love the members of his family had for one another. He is impressed with the happiness he is able to find in his past. Even now, he is warmed by those past experiences.

By three o'clock, he is feeling somewhat relaxed and begins to admire the wisdom of the old doctor. He is, however, shocked by the third slip, which reads, "Reexamine your motives." He becomes very defensive and rationalizes his pursuit of money, recognition, and success. After a while, though, a quiet voice inside him suggests that perhaps these motives are not good enough. He begins to recognize that an important aspect of alignment has been lost. In the past, his work had always been free and flowing when he felt like he was contributing something, making a sacrifice, rendering a service. However, as his work situation changed, he lost some of those feelings, and now feels entangled in the tentacles of the slow death process.

At six o'clock, he opens the last slip. It reads, "Write your worries in the sand." At this point, he sees the logic in the four thought-provoking statements. Getting outside himself, thinking about the happiness of the past, reflecting on the deep structure of the present, and eventually penetrating his own defenses allows him to reexamine and realign his own motives. Once he makes these internal adjustments, his external problems are less of an issue. If his motives, conscience, and capabilities are aligned, he will perform to his best ability, no matter what the external problem. Success is likely, but even if he experiences failures, he will have done the right things. In an important way, this man changes the world by changing himself.

REFLECTION AND DISCUSSION

➤ **Personal Steps to Change**

1. Identify some occasions when you were able to break the *logic of task pursuit.* What patterns do you see?

2. How might contemplation of the past help alter the future?

3. Explain what it means for a person to have the "wrong motives"? How might this occur in your life?

4. Describe a time when you were able to reexamine and realign your internal motives. What can you learn from reflecting on that experience? How does it apply to the present?

➤ **Organizational Steps to Change**

1. Do groups or organizations get trapped in the *logic of task pursuit?* Give an example.

2. The man in the story about the beach began to see making money, recognition, and success as the ultimate goal instead of by-products of doing the right things. This internal problem causes him to lose his sense of meaning, vitality, and drive. Can you think of a group or unit that may have lost its sense of meaning, vitality, and drive because of a similar distortion? Explain what happened and why.

3. Think of a group or unit that is important to you. How might you help the group or unit protect itself from losing vitality by becoming trapped in the logic of task pursuit?

4. If this group has already lost meaning, vitality, or drive because of a distorted sense of purpose, how might it be aided in realigning motives, conscience, and capabilities?

7

A New Perspective

Every morning for eleven years, Jason drove twenty miles to work. He felt that he intimately knew every aspect of the geography between those two locations. One day, his car was in the repair shop, and he drove his son's van to work. Jason was amazed at all the new things he saw. By sitting in a driver's seat nearly a foot higher than he was used to, he was able to see over fences, shrubs, and trees. There were all kinds of interesting "new" things to see. Our daily lives, like Jason's routine, are filled with structures that keep us from seeing more accurately. A change in perspective can greatly alter how we see and relate to the world.

Barriers to a New Perspective

Unfortunately, enlarging our perspective is very difficult. For one thing, the degree to which past successes have etched a given map, script, paradigm, or myth into our brain affects how we process information. They are extremely formidable barriers to tear down and replace. However, to gain insight into a new and challenging situation, these maps have to be reexamined.

Mary, for example, may have great dexterity with numbers. She receives a graduate degree in finance, graduates with honors, takes a job, and is quickly promoted into a management position. However, soon things begin to sour, and she gets negative evaluations.

People in her organization complain about her narrow focus and analytical interpersonal style. None of the complaints make sense to Mary. The negative feedback gets worse, and she concludes that the people in her work group are unfairly opposed to her.

In many ways, we all resemble Mary. Over time, everyone develops a formula for success. We get recognized and rewarded for our efforts. Positive experiences validate our worldview, map, script, myth, or paradigm. We know that we are all right—we have historical evidence to prove it.

What we fail to see is that our success by the old formula is like a map that has guided us to the edge of known territory. We cross a line into new territory and when we try to apply our old map there, strange and frustrating things happen. We get into a vicious cycle. We continue to explore our new and problematic territory with an old map, and that makes our problems worse. Our certainty that our old map must work drives us into a state of great pain and frustration. Only when our pain gets excruciating are we willing to humble ourselves and consider new actions that might allow us to successfully progress in our new situation.

Examining the Core Myths

Why do we sometimes need to find a new perspective? While our underlying worldview is fairly fixed, our external world is constantly changing. The two become increasingly out of synch, and the maps or paradigms that serve to guide our behavior become obsolete. When this happens, our known action plans will not work to our satisfaction in new situations. We have to reinvent ourselves so that we can meaningfully connect with our current world. This is not such a radical thought; it's actually an ongoing process. Deep change is, in fact, a reasonably common and ongoing experience necessary for internal development. In pursuing deep change, we redesign our maps or paradigms and realign ourselves with our surrounding environment. We reinvent ourselves by changing our perspective.

In considering the reinvention of our deeply held structures, McWhinney and Batista (1988) offer the concept of "remythologizing." They believe that our deep internal structures are myths or stories that order how we think. We have core or genesis myths that particularly influence us. Because our internal self gets out of alignment with our external world, we need to alter the self. One way to realign the self is to retell the most important stories in our life. Consider the following example.

> The Navajo Indians used their sand paintings in precisely this way to heal individuals who had become ill by being out of tune with their nature. The rituals, which lasted several days, centered on the telling of archetypal stories recalled in the sand paintings; this telling brought about a "cure" by bringing the patients into harmony with their natures. [p. 47]

This is a strange claim. What is going on? Over time, we lose touch with our inner self. Our core structures do not seem to integrate well with our current life demands. We go through the ritual of telling some core stories that are very central to our identity. When we repeat one of these stories, we do not retell it exactly. We recount it from the perspective of our current problem. It is presented in a unique way that allows us to reconnect our past foundation with our present and future structures. In fact, what we are really doing is realigning our past to include our present and future. We are combining them into one dynamic whole.

An Illustration of Remythologizing

Perhaps another illustration might be helpful. In my own attempt at continuous redefinition of the self, I engage in a weekly session of what I call soul writing. Sitting at my computer, I type a word at random and then freely associate a long list of words. The next step is to let my fingers write a sentence. I say fingers because I try to keep my mind out of the process. This is the time for my unconscious to express itself. I might write a poem or a descriptive paragraph or sometimes a brief story.

Several years ago, during my midlife crisis, I found myself crying while writing a short story. Tears were rolling down my cheeks. This had never happened before. This story, titled "The Prophecy," follows:

His chest was rotted out by tuberculosis and he was going to die. At 38 years of age, he was going to die.

He picked up the picture of his little girl. It was on the nightstand, next to the bed, where he lay. She was already dead. She had died over a year ago, a victim of encephalitis. Two years old, and he had watched them lower her into the ground.

As the hours passed, he tried to find some meaning in it all. What difference had he made? There was no money, no house, no insurance policy, only a wife with a new baby. Today she would bring the infant home. It was the only time he would ever see this child because this afternoon they were taking him to a hospital.

When they brought his wife home, she put the baby in the nursery before she went to see her husband. He had built the nursery for their first child but after she died he never went in again.

His wife helped him dress. The others helped him to the table. There was going to be a special lunch, then he would go.

When the meal was finished, and it was clearly time to leave, his wife helped him with his coat. He stood for a moment and then turned toward the nursery. She tried to help him but he waved his hand and she backed away.

In the nursery, he stood over the crib and watched the

little boy sleep. Finally, he bent over, held his tiny foot and kissed it.

When he came out, she looked at him expectantly. He spoke very softly. "I think our boy is going to make his mark on the world."

She bravely smiled. They helped him to the door. He stopped and embraced her. She kissed him and he left.

When I finished writing this story, it was very clear to me why I was crying. This story was very central to my own definition of self. I had heard this story many times while I was growing up. The storyteller was my mother; the dying man, my father. I was the newborn.

Each time my mother recounted the story, it was with great reverence. Her demeanor made it clear that this story was of sacred proportions. The story was etched into my consciousness. It is clearly a core myth.

Like the Indians in the cave, in writing this story I was retelling one of my core myths. Like the Indians, without knowing it, I was retelling the story from a new perspective. I had always heard the story from a woman who had lost her husband. Now I was telling the story from the point of view of a thirty-eight-year-old man who was dying. The man was asking himself what his life had meant. There was no money, no house, no insurance policy, no signs of worldly success, no legacy to mark his passage.

Years later, facing a midlife crisis, I was asking myself the very same questions about the meaning of my own life. Without even realizing it, I was trying to deal with the issues of impact and legacy. The day I wrote "The Prophecy," I let my subconscious speak. What legacy would I leave behind?

As all this became clear, I began to clarify what I wanted to do differently in my life. At work, for example, I took on a different perspective. I became more focused on my research. In my teaching and consulting, I became more caring yet more demanding. The resulting impact, in terms of outcome, was dramatic. I had a new perspective, and my life was changed. I became more empowered and more empowering.

New Perspective, New Energy

Our lives are always full of significant things about which we are unaware. Gaining an appreciation of these things can radically alter how we see the world and how we behave. When he was a sophomore in college, my son Ryan took an exciting internship with a Fortune 500 company. Ryan was given significant tasks, and he quickly realized that he could complete all of them successfully. He came home late each night, excited about his job. However, he was concerned that something else was happening to him, something he could not explain very well. He read a book about having purpose in life and concluded that he was losing his sense of perspective. He decided to do some personal values clarification. He made a list of questions about his values and his life direction and then spent a week writing answers in his journal.

At the end of the week, Ryan told me, "Dad, I have so much more energy. I'm doing all the same things I was doing before, but now I feel energized. I know what I want to accomplish in my life. I know what's important. I know why I'm doing the things I'm doing. All I've done is clarify who I am, but it makes all the difference. Now I'm doing everything with even more energy." Like Jason after driving the van, Ryan had gained a new perspective. He was seeing the world with new vision. His life activities now made more sense to him, and he had more energy for the process of living it.

➤ Personal Steps to Change

1. What does it mean to reinvent the self periodically, and why is this process necessary?

2. Think about someone you know well. Describe a script or myth that structures the behavior of that person.

3. Are there any scripts or myths that are very central to your identity? What positive and negative functions do they play in your life?

4. Give a brief description of the remythologizing process and how you might make use of it.

➤ Organizational Steps to Change

1. It has been argued that organizations, like people, have core myths that unconsciously structure behavior in the organization. Consider an organization that you know well, and identify a core myth. (You will recall that a myth is a collectively held story. It can be factually accurate or factually inaccurate.)

2. Over time, what have been the positive and negative functions of the core myth identified in Item 1?

3. Conceptualize a process that would help the organization engage in the process of remythologizing. What might be the potential risks and benefits of the process?

8

Confronting the Integrity Gap

Often when we evaluate a situation from a fresh perspective, it helps to clarify the actions we need to take. The resulting actions may present a series of risks. However, to initiate a deep change, we must confront a path littered by many risks and unforeseen challenges.

Professor William Torbert, at Boston College, teaches a self-examination technique to help his business students grow and develop. The approach includes writing descriptions of certain key personal experiences. The following example was written by one of his students, Steve Thompson, a project manager for an underwater pipeline construction company. Thompson describes a critical confrontation between himself and his boss, Ron Cedrick.

The Setting

Ron Cedrick is a unique man, not unlike George C. Scott's Patton, minus the .45-caliber pistols but wearing a shiny metal hard hat. He is famous. He had single-handedly tamed the seven seas through engineering and construction feats. He worked for himself and was in constant demand from the oil companies. He was to the offshore construction industry what Red Adair was to oil field fires. They traveled in the same circles, working for oil companies and commanding huge fees. The reason for his notoriety was simple: Ron Cedrick produced. No matter how difficult, the project always came in ahead of schedule.

The British National Oil Company (BNOC) had contracted with him to manage the construction and installation of its "single-anchor leg-mooring system." This system removed the need for flowing oil through hundreds of miles of pipeline from the offshore oil field to shore. Instead, the system enabled BNOC to fill its oil tankers in the oil field. The initial underwater construction had been completed in a deep, protected Norwegian fjord.

It was February in the North Sea: gray, cold, wet, and rough. At that time of year, the North Sea could be unpredictably violent. We were aboard a 600-foot derrick ship, saturation-diving to 540 feet. Saturation diving is a deep-sea diving procedure that enables two- to six-man diving teams to work at great depths without losing time for decompression. The divers, two per dive, work tethered from a diving submersible (bell) in a lightless, weightless, and hostile environment for periods of between eight and twelve hours per dive. Once the dive has been completed, the bell is winched back to the deck of the ship, where it is mated to dry, pressurized living chambers. The divers then remain pressurized until they are required to dive again.

The most dangerous part of this is the launch and recovery of the bell through the interface. The interface is the area between the deck of the ship and twenty-five feet below the surface of the water—the wave—affected region. This is the area where the bell is the most vulnerable. Rough seas have separated more than one diving bell from its winch cable. When this happens, there is usually little hope of rescuing the divers.

With this job, the work had been challenging and different. The saturation divers and topside crew were doing an outstanding job. Ron Cedrick was extremely pleased. This was of particular importance to me because it was my first job as project manager.

My Behavior

The wind had changed direction. I didn't like the looks of the sea. It looked like it does just before it really blows. The bell had just gone into the water for an anticipated twelve-hour dive.

After alerting the shift supervisor to "keep an eye on the weather," I went to the ship's bridge to have a look at the most recent weather forecast and facsimile. Ron Cedrick approached as I was reading the forecast that confirmed my suspicions. "You and your boys have done a real fine job. I appreciate that, and I know it will continue." He went on to explain that we had to complete the flow-line connection today in order to be ahead of schedule. He said, "I know that the weather's gettin' up a bit, but those boys respect you and will do what you ask—I've seen it. We need to keep that bell in the water just as long as we can before we let a little ol' weather shut us down."

"Yes, sir," I responded confidently. However, the outcome was all too predictable. I kept the bell in the water too long. The inclement weather turned into a gale. I pushed the diving operation beyond its safety limit. The recovery of the bell through twenty-foot seas was perilous. In the process, I not only compromised the safety of the divers but also set a poor precedent for the permissible operating parameters.

My Feelings

I had an overwhelming desire to succeed. That desire was manifested by my hard work, industriousness, and total task orientation. In defining or framing "success," I had identified not only successful task completion but also the satisfaction of Ron Cedrick as being synonymous with my success. After receiving positive feedback from Cedrick, I was torn between my responsibilities to my fellow workers and Cedrick's performance expectations.

The moment I reviewed the weather forecast, I became tense. I feared that I wouldn't have the strength of character to tell Cedrick that I'd have to shut down the operation. I was afraid that I'd have to deceive my people into thinking that pushing our safe operational limits was justified.

Finally, the awareness that I had manipulated my team and jeopardized the safety of the divers destroyed my illusion that I was an honest, ethical man. I received no satisfaction from the praise given me by Cedrick for "pulling it off." We had completed the flowline connection [Torbert, 1987, pp. 162–164].

According to Torbert, the writing exercise had allowed his student to identify an incongruity between his preferred self-image and his actual behavior. This process increases the capacity to perform in uncertain situations. That capacity is tied to integrity. The heart of effectiveness, Torbert argues, is building integrity through the constant observation of one's lack of integrity.

As Thompson continued to write such self-studies, he became increasingly aware of his responsibility, not only for the technical aspects of his work, but also for the "interpersonal, political, or ethical effects of his actions." Three months later, he took a higher position with a different firm at double his earlier salary. Three years later, he was a company president.

According to Torbert (1987), the most important lesson Thompson learned was that "there are a galaxy of responses to any situation." Torbert goes on to argue:

> Paradoxically, then, the method by which the manager expands his or her sense of responsibility to include long-run issues of legitimacy and integrity, as well as short-run issues of efficiency and middle-run issues of effectiveness, is to pay more attention to the many influences operating at the immediate moment of decision. The very sense of being stuck between two uncomfortable alternatives—the proverbial "rock and a hard place"—comes to be taken as a sign to listen more carefully for other voices. The manager then molds an original solution that does justice to the complex of influences, both implementing and testing the solution through action inquiry. . . . Most forms of professional knowledge result in conditional confidence—confidence that you will act well so long as the situation does not violate your assumptions about it. The active, awakening attention described here results in unconditional confidence—confidence that you are capable of discarding inaccurate assumptions and ineffective strategies in the midst of ongoing action. [p. 168]

The notion of unconditional confidence, described in Torbert's last sentence, is a hallmark of mastery in all areas of professional endeavor, particularly in the turbulent environment of higher-level management. It is the equivalent of the "capacity to get lost with confidence" mentioned earlier. In a world of constant change and uncertainty, unconditional confidence is a very desirable characteristic. Yet we see few examples of it.

Perhaps Torbert is unrealistic, or perhaps the price of unconditional confidence is so great that few people are willing to endure it. The concept of creating unconditional confidence is seldom taught in business schools or executive education programs. Maybe Torbert is really describing a spiritual discipline, and in the business world, we have great difficulty discussing such processes.

Ultimately, deep change, whether at the personal or the organizational level, is a spiritual process. Loss of alignment occurs when, for whatever reason, we begin to pursue the wrong end. This process begins innocently enough. In pursuing some justifiable end, we make a trade-off of some kind. We know it is wrong, but we rationalize our choice. We use the end to justify the means. As time passes, something inside us starts to wither. We are forced to live at the cognitive level, the rational, goal-seeking level. We lose our vitality and begin to work from sheer discipline. Our energy is not naturally replenished, and we experience no joy in what we do. We are experiencing slow death.

While the discourse of business tends to ignore the problem of slow death, in nearly all religions there is imagery for understanding this difficulty and a course toward its successful resolution. Contemplation is recommended to help us meet and overcome the challenges we face from our powerful defense mechanisms. Confronting our defense mechanisms leads to a necessary examination of self. To thwart our defense mechanisms and bypass slow death, we must confront first our own hypocrisy and cowardice. We must recognize the lies we have been telling ourselves. We must acknowledge our own weakness, greed, insensitivity, and lack of vision and courage. If we do so, we begin to understand the clear need for a course correction, and we slowly begin to reinvent our self. The transition is painful, and we are often hesitant, fearing that we lack the courage and confidence to proceed. We uncover a great paradoxical truth. Change is hell. Yet not to change, to stay on the path of slow death, is also hell. The difference is that the hell of deep change is the hero's journey. The journey puts us on a path of exhilaration, growth, and progress.

The hero finds strength, power, vitality, and energy in change. In experiencing deep change, our selfishness dies. Discipline and sensitivity are melded into one element and become our foundation. With this foundation, we have a new ability and unconditional confidence to influence others. In initiating deep change, we become aligned and revitalized because we are committed to the truth. We find the vision to empower both ourselves and our community. It would be useful if we could learn to communicate more comfortably about the process of deep change.

➤ Personal Steps to Change

1. What is your interpretation of the following statement? "Most forms of professional knowledge result in conditional confidence— confidence that you will act well so long as the situation does not violate your assumptions about it. The active, awakening attention described here results in unconditional confidence—confidence that you are capable of discarding inaccurate assumptions and ineffective strategies in the midst of ongoing action."

2. What is the relationship between unconditional confidence and the concept of leadership?

3. The arguments in this chapter suggest that integrity can be increased by the constant observation of our lack of integrity. How does the process of written self-study facilitate this process?

4. Outline a self-study program that might help you succeed at engaging your lack of integrity and improve your capacity to lead.

➤ Organizational Steps to Change

1. How does a group or unit lose integrity? Provide an example from your own organization.

2. In an organization, how do old scripts, myths, or paradigms contribute to the loss of integrity? Give an example.

3. Is it possible for a group or unit to be "capable of discarding inaccurate assumptions and ineffective strategies in the midst of ongoing action"? If so, provide an example. If you can't provide an

example, imagine a situation in which this might occur. Specify what would be necessary for it to occur.

4. With your response to Item 3 in mind, and given that most groups, units, and organizations cope with their lack of integrity by making the lack of integrity an undiscussable issue, how would you help a group move from denial to unconditional confidence?

9

Build the Bridge as You Walk on It

When we make the decision to initiate a change, we are facing a series of tough challenges. The path of change is often tortuous, with no clearly defined structure for determining if our action is right or wrong.

For several years, I worked with a fast-growing company that had made a variety of impressive accomplishments. At one point, I arranged for one of my students to write a case study about the company. I accompanied the student when the CEO was interviewed and recounted the first five years of the company.

It was an impressive story about the unfolding of a clear strategic plan. He described the company as moving effortlessly from phase A to B and then to C. This account did not match my understanding of what had taken place. I interjected and described a very different history. When he was challenged with the actual chaotic learning process that had taken place, he paused and then smiled and said, "It's true, we built the bridge as we walked on it."

Organizational and personal growth seldom follows a linear plan. This is an important principle to remember. When people recount a history of growth, they often tell it in a linear sequence, suggesting a rationality and control that never really existed.

When we have a vision, it does not necessarily mean that we have a plan. We may know where we want to be, but we will seldom know the actual steps we must take to get there. We must trust in ourselves to learn the way, to build the bridge as we walk on it. Deep change is an extensive learning process. When we pursue our vision, we must believe that we have enough courage and confidence in ourselves to reach our goal. We must leap into the chasm of uncertainty and strive bravely ahead.

Karl Weick tells a story about a military unit that was operating under difficult circumstances in the Alps during World War II. The commanding officer had sent a reconnaissance squad to scout out the surrounding area. A day passed, and the squad had not returned. It was feared that it was lost. Three days later, to everyone's relief, the squad returned. It had become lost and very discouraged when one of the men remembered that he had a map in his pack. This discovery brought a surge of hope and renewed energy. The squad leader took the map and led the squad safely back. The story was recounted to the relieved commanding officer, who summoned the squad leader to his tent and commended him for his fine work. It was not until later that the commanding officer noticed the map and realized that it was not a map of the Alps at all but one of the Pyrenees.

Weick points out that a good outcome can result from a flawed map. In this case, the map was a symbol that raised hope and energy. It allowed the squad leader to organize his men and get them to believe in a common strategy of action. The fact that the squad was again moving allowed the men to begin to calculate and think about where they were going. Even though their basic assumptions were wrong, the process of acting and calculating allowed them to learn and resolve their problem.

Deep change works in a similar way. Once we have our sense of direction, we need to get organized, pack our gear, get motivated, and move on out. This process introduces new information and allows us to make choices and progress and grow our way forward. The process also transmits signals to others, and they are attracted by our courage and motivation.

I am often reminded of Gandhi, early in his career, in South Africa. He had developed a vision and was working toward it. One day, a man arrived from another country and volunteered to join Gandhi. The man asked, "Aren't you surprised that I've shown up like this?" "No," Gandhi replied. He pointed out that when one discovers what is right and begins to pursue it, the necessary people and resources tend to turn up.

Trusting in our vision enough to start our journey into the chasm of uncertainty, believing that the resources will appear, can be very difficult. The fact that we have enough trust and belief in ourselves to pursue our vision is what signals to others that the vision is worth investing in. Our message is filled with integrity and good intentions. However, it is usually our actions, not our words, that send the message.

Acting on a vision that exceeds our resources is a test of our vision, faith, and integrity. Once C. K. Prahalad and I ran a strategic planning workshop for forty-two business school deans and their associates. They were a tough audience. They had little patience for our "theories." They wanted to get their strategic plans done.

We let them prepare their strategic plans and then provided some feedback. C. K. reviewed what he saw going on in many of the planning groups. They reviewed their resources, clarified their objectives, and then budgeted their resources for the upcoming period.

C. K. promised them that if all went well, they would be, at best, mediocre. Why? Because they were letting their present resources determine their future. They had plans, not visions. A vision would lead them toward a plan that exceeded their present resources.

His comments made the deans furious. Their level of denial and rejection soared. They accused us of being unrealistic and specified numerous constraints that made it unrealistic to think in the way that C. K. was suggesting. We listened for a long time. Finally, I asked if there were any business schools in the last ten years that had been transformed. They listed several. We chose one and analyzed the initial impossible situation it was in. We evaluated the strange and risky things that were undertaken by the dean of that particular school. Gradually, the complaints stopped, and the group began to show some interest in trying to understand what C. K. was saying.

Caught in a similar situation, most of us will react in exactly the same way. It is much easier and safer for us to stay within the zone of certainty, particularly if we are mired in the slow death dilemma and suffering. The challenges arise as we contemplate deep change. We must reach a point of ultimate despair and frustration before we seriously think about initiating deep change.

Tackling deep change and facing a new future, we must be willing to get lost with confidence. This confidence, along with tenacity, will guide our actions as we begin to build the bridge toward our vision. It is only when we experience deep change that the new vision comes into view. When we can actually "see" our vision, we must be willing to put it into action.

REFLECTION AND DISCUSSION

➤ Personal Steps to Change

1. After we take the hero's journey through uncertainty, we usually recount the story as if we always knew the ending and the steps that were needed to reach it. This retelling is a distortion of what really happened, and it misleads others into overrelying on a rational planning model. How does this process really unfold, and what does it mean to "build the bridge as we walk on it"? Provide an example from your own life.

2. Consider the lost army squad that was saved by the wrong map? How do the implications of this story apply to you?

3. Much has been said in this book about modeling change. What added insights can be derived from the following statement: "Trusting in our vision enough to start our journey into the chasm of uncertainty, believing that the resources will appear, can be very difficult. The fact that we have enough trust and belief in ourselves to pursue our vision is what signals to others that the vision is worth investing in. Our message is filled with integrity and good intentions. However, it is usually our actions, not our words, that send the message."

4. In what part of your life can you apply the concept of building the bridge as you walk on it?

➤ Organizational Steps to Change

1. "Building the bridge as you walk on it" suggests that an organization can engage in the process of learning while progressing under uncertainty. How often have you seen this process occur? Why doesn't it occur more frequently?

2. Consider the story of the business school deans. Identify a time when you have seen people in your organization behave in a similar manner. Describe what occurred.

3. Indicate how the modeling of the vision might solve a problem in your organization.

4. Like the army squad, is it possible for an organizational unit to become disoriented and get lost? If so, how could a leader use the implications arising from the army story in solving the problem?

Part III

Changing the Organization

10

Denying the Need for Change

An organization is a coalition of coalitions. In an elementary school, for example, there is a network composed of the student body; the teachers; the staff; the administration; the school board; the city, state, and national governments; the local taxpayers; and many other groups. Each of these may break down into smaller sets of coalitions, or they may temporarily combine with others to pursue a particular set of interests. The entire system is constantly evolving and changing.

Sometimes things are not as they seem. Organizations have publicly stated goals. These can usually be found in the published documents of the organization. The goal of the public school is to educate students. The goal of the manufacturing firm is to make and deliver high-quality products that people need. The goal of the hospital is to provide high-quality medical care. Behind these public goals, however, reside operative goals that often override the espoused public goals.

The operative goals are usually congruent with the interests of the dominant coalition. Consequently, we find that the public school actually exists, first, to serve the interests of the teachers' union or the administration and only secondarily to serve the interests of the students. The manufacturing firm first serves the personal interests of top management, and the hospital, the interests of the medical profession.

The publicly espoused constituency is sometimes the weakest of those that make up the organization. Parents do not have the knowledge, time, or skill to penetrate the protective bureaucracy of the public school system. Customers suffer a similar fate in getting the quality products or services they need. Patients are likewise often powerless in getting quality care.

Coalitions and the Pressure for Change

Several years ago, a major business leader who had made a dramatic turnaround in his company was invited to speak at a University of Michigan Business School faculty retreat. He spoke of the ever-increasing level of competition in business and the unending need to make significant organizational improvements to remain competitive. He discussed the sacrifices that his team had made to revolutionize the quality of the company's products and services. He also pointed out the financial success that resulted from their efforts.

At the conclusion of his address, we broke into small groups to discuss the applicability of his experience to our own strategic thinking for the school. In my group, the discussion turned to the irrelevance of his talk. He ran a business; we were a business school. The difference was immense. Great business schools are built by following a simple formula. The dean's job is to hire the finest research faculty in the world and then raise money to support their research. They, in turn, publish research. As a result, the school gains prestige and attracts even more resources and revenues, allowing the entire cycle to repeat.

This formula was not only sound but also sacred. It was the ultimate truth. Only an infidel would have dared to question it. By definition, then, any inquisitor would have been an infidel and not worth listening to. The logic was thus not only sound and sacred, it was what Chris Argyris would call "self-sealing" (Argyris, 1976, p. 16). That is, it could never be challenged, discussed, or tested.

Virtually every dominant coalition, in every organization, has a sacred and self-sealing model. It represents the most sacred of common belief patterns because it justifies the present behavior of the most powerful coalition. It justifies the current equilibrium and limits change to incremental rather than transformational efforts.

External Change Processes

Several years ago, *Business Week* magazine initiated a new approach to the evaluation of business schools. It took the concept of the customer seriously. The magazine polled recent business school graduates and active recruiters. The evaluation had little to do with academic research productivity. At issue was the quality of a business school education and the quality of the graduate as a job candidate.

There were some surprising results. The hierarchy of the reputed "top" business schools was altered. Some of these schools did not even make the top twenty entries, and other schools improved their rankings dramatically.

I remember talking with a dean from one of the "top" schools that had dropped completely from the top twenty. The impact on him was tremendous. Suddenly, the university president was asking him difficult and probing questions. Donors began withdrawing their support, and the student population was outraged. He faced a multitude of problems. He felt that the *Business Week* survey was unjust and that the methodology used was unsound. A few months later, he resigned.

The results of this survey were evaluated at the next meeting of the department chairs at the Michigan Business School. Michigan had been ranked sixth. The recruiters had given us a strong assessment, but our graduates were not as kind. During the meeting, someone suggested that all that the students were really interested in was obtaining jobs, so we should simply hire another person in the placement office. Several other faculty members supported the position.

I, however, disagreed and offered an alternate view. I suggested that the students were voicing a much deeper concern. They were angry that the business school was, for them, not a learning community. They felt that it was a factory and that they were treated like widgets on an assembly line. They were a necessary evil. Their tuition dollars were the necessary resources that allowed the professors—the dominant coalition—to engage in the activities that brought them the most significant individual rewards—research and publication. At the most basic level, the students were not objects of reverence but rather a bothersome distraction. The implicit goal for the dominant coalition was to spend as little time with them as possible.

It does not take long for us to discover how others feel about us. When we are not treated with respect, we become angry. The business students, I argued, were calling for a fundamental alteration in the system; they wanted a deep change. They wanted to be treated as students in an educational community, not widgets on an assembly line. They wanted a system designed to meet their needs. They were telling us that they wanted a deep change.

There was a marked silence. Attention was quickly shifted back to the notion of putting an additional person in placement. When a system faces the challenge to make a deep change, individuals will usually create an alternative scenario. It is usually the scenario of the painless fix. It is an early stop on the road to slow death.

Two years later, Business Week repeated the survey. This time, Michigan fell from sixth to seventh. On the surface, this was a fairly insignificant change and might have been easily ignored. There was one problem, however. One of the schools that had dropped dramatically in the original survey had decided to invest heavily in the change process. Consequently, that school was now ranked number one.

Michigan faced a challenge. What if, during the next two years, ten schools decided to make deep changes in their educational processes? This was a difficult question for our business school. If we did not make any changes in our processes, we would risk dropping further down in the rankings. The repercussions could be enormous.

Suddenly, for Michigan, as well as for all the other major business schools, the very core of the school was in danger. The presence of this risk led us to the decision that we must undertake deep change.

As a result, the curriculum and everything associated with our educational process was realigned. Stress levels soared as our faculty and staff faced the necessity of altering and eliminating many of the structures that were part of their daily work routine. Experimental processes and programs were instituted. Tough decisions were made under pressure, frequently on strategies with uncertain outcomes. We encountered many difficult situations and frequent heated discussions. It seemed as if we were always attending meetings. People found it extremely difficult, if not impossible, to fulfill all of their responsibilities. In the middle of one very painful meeting, one person passed a note to me that said, "Change sucks!" That simple expression of frustration captures an important point. Deep change throughout a system means sacrifice and suffering for everyone. It also means engaging in real conflict. It is not very pleasant.

As many of our initial experiments in converting our programs showed signs of success, we became increasingly proud of our efforts. We were seeing positive results from our hard work that gave us a sense of personal achievement and pride in our institution. Naturally, we were all assuming that when the next *Business Week* poll was released, our great efforts would be recognized. They were—we climbed from seventh place to fifth. That may seem a small reward for all our efforts. However, a significant change had taken place. After the second poll, many of the top schools recognized the risk of not making any changes. Our competitors were also realigning their programs. The rules had changed.

Internally Driven Change

Organizations are coalitional. The dominant coalition in an organization is seldom interested in making deep change. Hence deep change is often, but not always, driven from the outside. In the future, great business schools will still be built by hiring great researchers, but they are also likely to be expected to meet the needs of other constituencies. This will mean that they will have to meet a wider and often competing set of expectations. Competition and the motivation for survival will remain intense.

Many critics of universities will agree with the foregoing analysis and point with disdain at the behavior of professors. I do the same when I read critiques of doctors, lawyers, politicians, executives, and others. In pointing at others, however, I take a dangerous position. Why? Because the story of the business schools is not very different from the story told by the business leader at our retreat. Nor is it different from the stories told to me by hospital administrators, public administrators, or leaders of volunteer organizations. Although each thinks that the experiences being related are unique, all are disclosing a story of survival in an increasingly turbulent and competitive environment. We all face the deep change or slow death dilemma.

REFLECTION AND DISCUSSION

➤ Personal Steps to Change

1. Identify some situations in which you have confronted a dominant coalition.

2. Identify some strategies for influencing a dominant coalition.

3. Consider the story of the business school and how it changed. Generate a strategy, based on this story, that would solve a problem in your life.

➤ Organizational Steps to Change

1. List the major coalitions in your organization.

2. Determine the dominant coalition in your organization, and give an example of how your organization first serves the dominant coalition.

3. Specify the sacred logic for the dominant coalition in your organization.

11

Finding the Source of the Trouble

I know of a company that was forced to downsize. The CEO recognized that in addition to downsizing, the company also needed to eliminate work from the system. He argued that downsizing without an accompanying plan to remove tasks from the system would merely result in workforce burnout.

At the start of the downsizing process, the CEO delivered a clear message to every member of the organization. He pointed out that a large amount of work must be eliminated. He made it clear that the only activities that could not be cut out were those that were required by law, necessary for ethical reasons, or absolutely essential to organizational survival.

This CEO's comments were well received. Everyone agreed that work must be eliminated and that there were a lot of extraneous procedures in the system. Despite this agreement, however, after twelve months, little work had been eliminated. Indeed, everyone agreed that the workload had increased. Why?

The Influence of the Implicit

Organizational cultures are not designed; they tend to evolve naturally. At any given time, the culture will facilitate certain desired outcomes and block others. The CEO in the downsizing example encouraged everyone to eliminate work from the system. He had the most formal power in his organization, and he offered a plausible strategy. Everyone agreed his advice was wise and desirable. Yet a year later, everyone was doing even more work. Despite the CEO's power and strategy, change did not naturally follow.

Organizational cultures tend to be like Joel Chandler Harris's Tar Baby: Though culture is malleable, it is also very sticky and difficult to deal with. When a seemingly rational strategy conflicts with an existing set of implicit governing rules, little change occurs. In this case, the organization's implicit governing rules took precedence over the CEO's explicit directive. Eliminating work from the system required a much deeper kind of change—a deep change that was not initiated by the CEO's directive.

The Problem: Often in a Surprising Place

In his book *Zen and the Art of Motorcycle Maintenance*, Robert Pirsig (1974) comments on the concept of hierarchy. He points out that the elements of a hierarchy tend to be maintained, even if they have lost all meaning and purpose. As a result, many people spend their lives completing meaningless tasks—not because of some bad person but because the system is no longer functioning in a productive manner. The problem, he argues, is that the system is very formidable. No one is willing to take on the responsibility of changing the system.

One of Pirsig's key insights is into the area of where the problem actually resides. He writes:

> But to tear down a factory or to revolt against a government or to avoid repair of a motorcycle because it is a system is to attack effects rather than causes; and as long as the attack is upon effects only, no change is possible. The true system, the real system, is our present construction of systematic thought itself, rationality itself, and if a factory is torn down but the rationality which

produced it is left standing, then that rationality will
simply produce another factory. If a revolution destroys
a systematic government, but the systematic patterns of
thought that produced that government are left intact,
then those patterns will repeat themselves in the succeeding government. There is so much talk about the
system. And so little understanding. [p. 88]

The problem is not "out there" but inside each one of us. The
external "system" that we often complain about actually exists
within each of us. Our concept of hierarchy is a product of the way
we think. As rational beings and an important part of our organization's systems, we continually propagate and preserve the structures of the various systems by our daily behavior.

Within our organizations, we have spent many years learning
how to routinize and control things, how to build equilibrium-
preserving hierarchies. Though we are skilled at creating hierarchical cultures, we are very unskilled at altering organizational structures
that have outlived their usefulness. Though today the rhetoric of
organization calls for nonhierarchical approaches, our existing cognitive maps still drive us toward maintaining the old culture.

Once we support the organizational structure, we are tied to its
preservation. We deny the need for change and increase our commitment to the problem. For example, one Fortune 500 company
was in the midst of a difficult time when a rumor spread that the
corporation was going to use its sizable political clout to "go after"
its critics. Shortly afterward, an employee who was taking a night
class at our school told his instructor that he had been told to report
any professor who criticized the corporation, and appropriate action
would be taken.

I found it interesting that given the depth of the change that
the external world was demanding from this organization, it could
afford to invest any energy or resources in an attempt to "police"
the extensive criticism it was receiving. Though the energy

investment seemed unwise, it was in fact not unlike what many of us do at the personal level. We use our authority to cut off criticism rather than confront the facts that would suggest that we need to change.

Why Change Does Not Happen

Suppose, however, that things get so bad that a call for change can no longer be policed or ignored. What happens? A directive for change is initiated but fails. Why? One reason can be found in Pirsig's observation about the tearing down of an old system. It has to do with the unconscious map in us. We can tear down all the hierarchies, but they will all reappear because no matter what we utter, at the behavioral level, we continue to enact the old map.

At the organizational level the same thing occurs. Consider, for example, the process of downsizing. An organization may eliminate a quarter of its workforce. Initially, the financial statement looks better. After a time, however, the same old problems resurface, and again the workforce is trimmed. Soon the outdated system goes out of existence. Why? Because the source of the problem, the old map, continues to drive the behavior of those who are left. That is, the old governing rules are still in place. The workforce has been cut, but the strategic plan is still inadequate or sales and finance are still at war. Like Pirsig's description of hierarchy, the original patterns of behavior remain in our cognitive maps, and we continue to use them.

After downsizing, for example, the remaining players usually return to the patterns that existed before the downsizing effort. Though it is true that some systems need to be leaner, nearly all systems need to be more responsive. In our world of hyperchange, if the organizational culture, the deep structure, does not change, downsizing is only a short-term financial fix. It does not address the real problem. The real problem just keeps re-enacting itself.

The CEO who encouraged taking work out of the system was very wise in calling for exactly what was needed. But he was not successful in bringing about organizational change. Despite his directive, the organization's governing rules were unaffected. Deep change requires more than the identification of the problem and a call for action. It requires looking beyond the scope of the problem and finding the actual source of the trouble. The real problem is frequently located where we would least expect to find it, inside ourselves. Deep change requires an evaluation of the ideologies behind the organizational culture. This process happens only when someone cares enough to exercise the courage to uncover the issues no one dares to recognize or confront. It means someone must be enormously secure and courageous. Culture change starts with personal change. We become change agents by first altering our own maps. Ultimately, the process returns us to the "power of one" and the requirement of aligning and empowering oneself before successfully changing the organization.

➤ Personal Steps to Change

1. After reflecting on the quote from Pirsig, indicate some applications of his statement to situations in your own life.

2. Indicate some examples in which you have cut off flows of criticism rather than confront the need to change.

3. Elaborate on the statement, "Culture change starts with personal change."

➤ Organizational Steps to Change

1. Consider the CEO who directed that work be eliminated. Describe a similar situation in your organization.

2. "Organizational cultures are not designed; they tend to evolve naturally. At any given time, the culture will facilitate certain desired outcomes and block others. The CEO in the downsizing example encouraged everyone to eliminate work from the system. He had the most formal power in his organization, and he offered a plausible strategy. Everyone agreed that his advice was wise and desirable. Yet a year later, everyone was doing even more." Explain how some of the governing rules in your organization work to preserve the status quo.

3. "Within our organizations, we have spent many years learning how to routinize and control things, how to build equilibrium-preserving hierarchies. Though we are skilled at creating hierarchical cultures, we are very unskilled at altering organizational structures that have outlived their usefulness. Though today the rhetoric of organization calls for nonhierarchical approaches, our existing

cognitive maps still drive us toward maintaining the old culture."
Provide an illustration of this statement.

4. "After downsizing, the remaining players usually return to the
patterns that existed before the downsizing effort." Identify a
serious problem that is embedded in the governing rules of your
organizational culture. What do you think it would take to resolve
the problem?

5. Reflect on your response in Item 4. Does it assume action on your
part, or does your response suggest powerlessness? If it suggests
powerlessness, is there any way to reconceptualize the response
so that you are playing an empowered role?

12

When Success Is the Engine of Failure

I once interviewed a man who worked for a large company. He described a problem and his eventual personal transformation. After graduating from a five-year engineering program in four years, he had taken a job with his current organization. This engineer was seen as a technically competent, innovative, and action-oriented person and was promoted several times. After his last promotion, however, he went through several difficult years. For the first time, he received serious negative feedback, his ideas and proposals were regularly rejected, and he was passed over for promotion. In reflection, he said:

> It was awful. Everything was always changing, yet nothing ever seemed to happen. The people above me would sit around forever and talk about things. The technically right answer didn't matter. They were always making what I thought were wrong decisions, and when I insisted on doing what was right, they got angry and would ignore what I was saying. Everything was suddenly political. They would worry about what everyone was going to think about every issue—how you looked, attending cocktail parties. That stuff to me was unreal and unimportant.

This man faced a classic career problem. Upon entering the realm of upper management, he found that his technical models and hard-edged strategies were no longer working. The personal participation and political involvement required were antithetical to everything he believed. During this time, his underlying cognitive map failed him. Finally, a critical incident occurred. Like many critical incidents in the search for self, this incident may seem comical to an outside observer.

On several occasions, the engineer's boss commented that he was very impressed with one of the engineer's subordinates. His boss indicated that no matter how early he himself arrived at work, this man's car was always in the parking lot.

The engineer went to visit the subordinate who had been singled out. After some questioning, the man explained, "I have four teenagers who wake up at dawn for paper routes, athletic practice, and other activities. The mornings at my house are chaotic, so I come in early. I read for a while, write in my journal, read the paper, have some coffee, and then start work at eight."

When the engineer left the man's office, he was furious that his subordinate should be given such high praise for behaviors that had nothing to do with his commitment to the organization. After a moment, however, he began to laugh. The gap between perception and reality suddenly seemed hysterical. He later said, "That was when I discovered perception. From that point forward, everything started to change." Eventually he came to appreciate the need to think and operate in more complex ways within the higher levels of the organization. He describes the process as follows:

> I went through some terrible years. I occasionally thought I had reached my level of incompetence, but I refused to give up. In the end, the frustration and pain turned out to be positive things because they forced me to consider some alternative perspectives. I eventually

learned that there were other realities besides the technical reality.

I discovered perception and long time lines. At higher
levels, what matters is how people see the world, and
everyone sees it a little differently. Technical facts are
not as available or as important. Things change more
rapidly at higher levels. You are no longer buffered from
the outside world. Things are more complex, and it takes
longer to get people on board. I decided I had to be a lot
more receptive and a lot more patient. It was an enormous adjustment, but then things started to change. I
think I became a much better manager.

This man had undergone a classic personal transformation. From
his new perspective, everything had a different meaning. He had
changed how he viewed himself and his world. It was a deep
change—not unlike a religious conversion.

Roles and Paradigms

Like the man in the story I just recounted, many of us enter an organization and apply our efforts toward succeeding as an individual
contributor. Typically, if we are successful, we are promoted to the
role of a manager. In making this change, we are often required to
alter our paradigm or worldview. We transition from what I call the
paradigm of technical competence to the paradigm of political
transaction.

The Individual Contributor and the Paradigm of Technical
Competence

The paradigm of technical competence is detailed in the second
column of Table 12.1. This table illustrates two of three basic paradigms of organization life. (The third paradigm will appear in

Chapter Fourteen.) The first premise of the paradigm of technical competence is personal survival. This does not mean that the individual does not take the needs of others into account. It means that ultimately one has to take care of oneself, and basically, all decisions follow this premise. This first premise is an implicit but potent driver of behavior.

The individual contributor views the organization as a system of technical production. The ultimate source of power comes from the competence to get the job done correctly. Credibility is determined by some specific professional standards, such as the principles of accounting or the accomplishment of a measurable goal, such as the number of sales.

Individual contributors are often cynical about management, seeing managers as bureaucrats who frequently block progress. This cynicism often grows because individual contributors tend to rely on rational confrontation, the communication of facts, and other simple influence strategies to persuade those in authority. These strategies often fail to bring change, and frustration keeps increasing. The political environment in an organization is very difficult for the individual contributor.

The individual contributor is frequently a rational and tactical planner. The technical norms of the profession underscore conventional patterns of behavior. This paradigm of technical competence typically arises during professional training and is usually reinforced by the technical orientation that is rewarded in early career positions.

The Manager and the Paradigm of Political Transaction

The paradigm of technical competence made the engineer in our story successful. His success brought a promotion into management. As a manager, he faced a lot of frustration. His new role as manager required an expansion of consciousness, a new way of seeing and being. The engineer, as a manager, eventually experienced a deep change and internalized the paradigm of political transaction.

Table 12.1. Two Paradigms of Organizational Life.

	Individual Contributor Technical Paradigm	Manager Transactional Paradigm
First objective	Personal survival	Personal survival
Nature of organization	Technical system	Political system
Source of power	Technical competence	Effective transactions
Source of credibility	Technical standards	Organizational position
Orientation to authority	Cynical	Responsive
Orientation to elite	Rational confrontation	Compromise
Orientation to planning	Rational-tactical	Rational-strategic
Communication patterns	Factual	Conceptual
Strategic complexity	Simple	Complex
Behavior patterns	Conventional	Conventional
Ease of understanding	Comprehensible	Comprehensible
Source of paradigm	Professional training	Administrative socialization

Underlying the paradigm of political transaction is the same basic premise found in the paradigm of technical competence: personal survival or self-interest. When an individual transitions to the paradigm of political transaction, the person is still concerned with professional survival. The rest of the paradigm, however, differs considerably from the first.

In the paradigm of political transaction, the organization is not only a technical system but also a political system. People are seen as continually exchanging resources—gaining and losing power in the perpetual process of negotiation. This paradigm recognizes that individuals, and coalitions of individuals, who make the most efficient, competitive, and effective transactions gain the most power. The organization is a system of exchange.

In trying to bring change, a person with this paradigm is likely first to employ strategies of rational persuasion, telling people what they need to do differently. If this fails, they are likely then to turn to strategies of political leverage, using various forms of coercion to bring change. When dealing with authoritarian figures, this paradigm suggests that it is important to compromise—maintaining relationships and avoiding career risks.

If the individual contributor learns the paradigm of technical competence in school, the manager learns the political paradigm at work. Technical success eventually brings the individual contributor to the point where a new paradigm is required. At that point, further career success is predicated on transitioning into the very different paradigm of political transaction.

Learning how to act appropriately and to cope effectively in the political environment is extremely important. It is critical to survival in an organization. Understanding and embracing the political paradigm can be difficult for the individual contributor. It often requires a deep change.

➤ **Personal Steps to Change**

1. The engineer in this chapter was well trained and very successful, yet something went wrong. "Upon entering the realm of upper management, he found that his technical models and hard-edged strategies were no longer working." Explain the man's technical paradigm and why it made him first a success and then a failure.

2. Identify a similar experience in your life.

3. From your life experience, what are the strengths and weaknesses of the paradigm of political transaction?

➤ **Organizational Steps to Change**

1. How often do people in your organization go through processes similar to the experience described in this chapter? Give some examples.

2. Are there other personal changes that predictably occur in your organization?

3. When people are going through personal paradigm changes, their effectiveness tends to decline, and the organization incurs a cost. What is done in your organization to help people make deep personal change? Are there additional courses of action that might be possible?

4. Like the engineer, there may be people around you that are feeling lonely and desperate as they go through a deep personal change. Identify some of these people. Make a list of some helpful actions you could take.

13

The Tyranny of Competence

An individual contributor is a person whose technical competence is judged in terms of singular rather than interdependent action. The more unique the individual output, the more powerful the person becomes. The overapplication of the technical paradigm by an individual can lead to a negative state called the tyranny of competence.

The Individual Contributor and the Tyranny of Competence

As a young boy, one of my heroes was Ted Williams. Ted played left field for the Boston Red Sox and was one of the greatest hitters of all time. He was also an individualist. His career was strewn with indicators of his nonconformity. He shot pigeons off the wall in Fenway Park, refused to engage in the traditional tip of the hat after a home run, refused to wear a tie, was always at war with the press, and generally insisted on being his own person.

Ted's individualism added to his mystique. When I was young, I read a book published by *Sports Illustrated*. The book contained a two-paragraph story on Williams. It went something like this.

There were two Harvard types sitting behind the dugout in Fenway Park. They were drinking beer, discussing the individualism of Ted Williams, and offering theories as to how he got away with what he did. They were deeply enmeshed in the conversation when they were interrupted by a blue-collar type sitting behind them. "You guys are missing the whole point. Williams gets to be Williams because everyone wants to be who he is. Secretly, everyone wants to be so good at his job that he can tell his boss to go to hell and his boss has to take it. Everyone wants to be Ted Williams."

The two Harvard types thought briefly about it, looked at each other, and nodded approvingly. They turned to the man, offered him a beer, and asked him to join them.

It is fairly easy to find an extraordinarily competent person who plays a particularly powerful role in an organization. It can be an administrative assistant who knows where every critical file is located, a programmer who is the only one who knows how to write a particular kind of code, or a salesperson with the unique skills necessary to sell a particular product.

While it is very important that people have such competence, competence tends to be the single most important thing to an individual contributor who holds the paradigm of technical competence. This person often argues, "The only thing that should matter here is how well someone does the job." Organizations definitely need people who are technically competent. This view is logically sound; however, it can lead to a few problems.

From this perspective, competence often comes to mean task completion—finding the file or making the sale. Often people who are uniquely skilled to complete a given task are quick to point out the inability of others to do what they do. Vocalizing this point gives them a sense of power. At lower levels, the organization often rewards and reinforces this position.

In the extreme cases, the paradigm of technical competence becomes the tyranny of competence. A powerful individual contributor takes control and then begins to undermine the influence of others. The work climate is poisoned, and morale declines. Cooperation turns to competition, then ill will, and then into subtle forms of sabotage. Yet seldom does anyone vocalize or communicate the problem. If the problem manages to surface, the issues of relationships and teamwork are downplayed or neutralized.

The arguments for competence are powerful and often overshadow or mask a problem area. An example of such an argument is the comment along the lines of "We couldn't survive without Mary. No one else can sell that thing, and it represents 30 percent of our business." This statement is often so self-evident that no one thinks to point out that the cooperative effort that should be the essence of the organization has already ceased to survive. People come to work, but there is a lack of communication, commitment, and cooperation. The process of slow death has set in.

In one organization, a man of enormous technical competence was allowed to gain a lot of power, and many of his actions poisoned the climate in the workplace. People around him hated to come to work and went to great lengths to avoid dealing with him. Their bad feelings, irrationality, and inefficiencies were costing the organization large but undocumented sums of money. Finally, the situation grew so bad that people united and demanded change. A senior person intervened in this tyranny of competence and tried to coach the man. The recipient found the feedback incomprehensible and argued that he was doing his "job" better than anyone else in the place. The organization was simply out to get him for personal and political reasons.

Note the accuracy of his argument. He was doing his "job" well, and the organization was out to get him for political and personal reasons. The problem was in his definition of the word *job*. His job did not include relating to other people. Organizational relationships, with their interactions and political processes, are as real as physical objects. Not disciplining oneself enough to maintain good relationships is, in fact, destructive behavior.

This man eventually left his job, convinced that he had been politically rejected (which was correct) for unjust reasons (which was incorrect). The day he went down the stairs for the last time, people came out of their offices, held hands, spontaneously danced, and sang, "Ding dong, the wicked witch is dead!" They discovered that this irreplaceable person was indeed replaceable. The top executives marveled at the resulting increase in overall performance. They vowed not to make the same mistake again.

Some organizations remain blind to the tyranny of competence. I know of an organization that prides itself on hiring only the brightest and most competent people. This organization has grown fairly large. It now requires leadership from people other than just the original entrepreneur. There are competent individuals throughout the organization who do their jobs as well as anyone in the world. However, they do not function as a cohesive team; in fact, they have trouble comprehending the concept of teamwork. As a result, the organization experiences the tyranny of competence at many levels and is choosing slow death. An enlightened and thriving organization contains competent people whose jobs are not defined or evaluated solely in terms of technical task completion.

I know a man who has acquired many organizations. He once explained to me that one of his first actions in acquiring a new organization is to identify the indispensable people. If they are not team players, the first thing he does is replace them. If they are team players, he gives them a date by which they are to have trained one or more people to do their jobs. He refuses to become a victim of the tyranny of competence.

If Ted Williams had been traded, my young heart would have been broken. However, I now wonder if any of his individual batting titles might have been exchanged for a victorious trip by his team to the World Series. For many years, people have talked of the "Curse of the Bambino." People believe that the Red Sox are cursed and cannot win a World Series because they once traded Babe Ruth. For at least one period, the real curse may have been valuing technical competence to the point of choosing collective failure.

➤ Personal Steps to Change

1. Provide an argument in favor of the paradigm of technical competence.

2. Provide an argument against the paradigm of technical competence.

3. Identify the assumptions you employ in trying to obtain power and influence.

➤ Organizational Steps to Change

1. Organizations must have technically competent people. What does your organization do to find and obtain such people?

2. What insights do you derive from the following statement? "In the extreme cases, the paradigm of technical competence becomes the tyranny of competence. A powerful individual contributor takes control and then begins to undermine the influence of others. The work climate is poisoned, and morale declines. Cooperation turns to competition, then ill will, and then into subtle forms of sabotage. Yet seldom does anyone vocalize the problem. If the problem manages to surface, the issues of relationships and teamwork are downplayed or neutralized."

3. "In one organization, a man of enormous technical competence was allowed to gain a lot of power, and many of his actions poisoned the climate in the workplace. People around him hated to come to work and went to great lengths to avoid dealing with him. Their bad feelings, irrationality, and inefficiencies were

costing the organization large but undocumented sums of money."
Why, in such a case, did no one take action?

4. Provide two arguments, one for and one against the following
   strategy: "I know a man who has acquired many organizations. He
   once explained that one of his first actions in acquiring a new
   organization was to identify the indispensable people. If they were
   not team players, the first thing he did was replace them. If they
   were team players, he gave them a date by which they were to
   have trained one or more people to do their jobs. He refused to
   become a victim of the tyranny of competence."

14

The Internally Driven Leader

Several years ago, I was asked to design a new M.B.A. course on leadership, vision, and change. In doing so, I took an unusual approach. Half of the class sessions would be devoted to case studies. The cases were written on several recent dramatic organizational transformations. The leader of each transformation was invited to make a presentation. The other half of the class sessions would be based on movies that depicted the efforts of transformational leaders to effect organizational change. The students would view the movies at home and come to class prepared to discuss them as cases of change.

It was exciting for the students to have actual business leaders answering questions about the changes the leaders had spearheaded. While business leaders were often inspiring, their sessions turned out not to be the most important part of the class. The movies proved more instructive. The business cases were usually washed clean of conflict, failure, and error. They were stories told by companies for public consumption. In contrast, the movies allowed me to guide the students through crucial behavioral issues they would not encounter in normal case studies.

One of the first movies we covered was *Brubaker,* the story of a warden who attempted to transform a totally corrupt prison in the southern United States. Brubaker pursued a vision of deep change that threatened the existing political coalitions inside and outside the prison. Each step he took caused more intense resistance. This resistance extended all the way to the governor's office.

Within that office, Brubaker had an ally named Lillian. At the height of the controversy, she phoned several times to tell him that he must relent and begin negotiation. If he would be realistic and practical, he could get the resources he needed to improve the physical conditions inside the prison. Brubaker replied, "Every warden puts new paint on the walls." He argued that in making deep change one might "compromise on strategy but never on principle." After engaging in some highly controversial activities that made deep changes in the system, Brubaker was fired.

When this case is reviewed by my M.B.A. students, they nearly always conclude that Brubaker was a failure. He should have listened to Lillian. After some discussion, I point out that after he left, the prisoners grasped what Brubaker was trying to do and sued the state. The court ordered the prison closed or reformed. Was Brubaker successful? My students do not think so. If he was fired, he was, by definition, a failure. In considering organizational change, the contrasting views of Lillian and Brubaker are worth further consideration.

The Political and Transformational Paradigms

Lillian and Brubaker each held an implicit theory on organization and change. Lillian's theory is held by most managers. It is the paradigm of political transaction. (We were briefly introduced to this paradigm earlier and will consider it more fully in a moment.)

Brubaker also held an implicit theory on organization and change, the transformational paradigm. It is embraced by very few managers. Interestingly, Brubaker's theory seems to be reflected in the behavior of every one of the transformational leaders that we observe during the semester. Let's examine the differences between these two worldviews (see Table 14.1.).

Table 14.1. Three Paradigms of Organizational Life.

	Individual Contributor Technical paradigm	Manager Transactional paradigm	Leader Transformational paradigm
First objective	Personal survival	Personal survival	Vision realization
Nature of organization	Technical system	Political system	Moral system
Source of power	Technical competence	Effective transactions	Core values
Source of credibility	Technical standards	Organizational position	Behavioral integrity
Orientation to authority	Cynical	Responsive	Self-authorizing
Orientation to elite	Rational confrontation	Compromise	Complex confrontation
Orientation to planning	Rational-tactical	Rational-strategic	Action learning
Communication patterns	Factual	Conceptual	Symbolic
Strategic complexity	Simple	Complex	Highly complex
Behavior patterns	Conventional	Conventional	Unconventional
Ease of understanding	Comprehensible	Comprehensible	Nearly incomprehensible
Source of paradigm	Professional training	Administrative socialization	Personal rebirth

The paradigms are not mutually exclusive. Each one accepts the previous paradigm(s). Lillian's is an example. Her fundamental assumption was personal survival. She believed that it was necessary to compromise with individuals in power so that she could maintain her position and continue her career. Unlike the engineer in Chapter Twelve, she saw the organization not only as a technical system but also as a political system. She understood the less complex technical paradigm.

The transactional paradigm suggests that an organization is a coalition of political interests. Everyone has an agenda and a set of needs and is engaged in a variety of transactions where a wide array of resources are exchanged. Power accrues to the person who makes the most effective transactions. From this perspective, it is important to continue up a hierarchical career path. The higher one travels up the organizational chart, the more responsibilities and rewards there are. When people hold this kind of mind-set, they tend to be very responsive to authority figures. When conflicts emerge involving power elites, people holding the political transactional paradigm take a diplomatic orientation and resolve controversial issues by using compromise. Their planning processes are both rational and strategic. Their patterns of communication are strategic.

The transactional paradigm arises from administrative socialization. An organization informally teaches its members this paradigm. Remember the engineer and his very difficult transition. His difficulties were a result of trying to survive within the organization while learning the complexities and nuances of the transactional paradigm.

Brubaker's behavior reflects a more complex set of implicit assumptions. These are held by most transformational leaders. The first assumption of the transformational paradigm is the most radical and the hardest to understand. This paradigm does not assume personal survival but instead vision realization at any cost. If the vision lives and thrives, it does not matter if the leader is fired, assassinated, or humiliated. The vision itself is far more important than personal survival.

Under the transformational paradigm, the organization is viewed not just as a technical or a political system but also as a moral system. There are certain values and principles that are more powerful than the political interests of any particular coalition.

A transformational leader will develop a plan of action, mobilize the workforce, and unleash power by vocalizing the core values of the system. Their source of credibility is their behavioral integrity. A leader must walk the walk and talk the talk. Every action must be in alignment with the vision. To fail on this dimension is to reduce the vision to an exercise in hypocrisy. When evaluating a vision, people watch the behavior of their leaders and quickly recognize if a leader lacks personal discipline and commitment. People know when a leader's words are empty, and they respond by simply ignoring the vision until the vision dies.

When it comes to authority, the leader is self-authorizing. Unlike the manager who has internalized the organization, the leader understands the external boundaries and restrictions but selects another path. The leader chooses to be free. This transformational perspective arises from a deep inner reflection about the self and the internal and external structures that determine the organizational systems. The leader understands the organization's systems in a way that cannot be understood within the framework of the paradigm of political transaction. Hence when a confrontation emerges, the leader often engages in a series of very complex strategies that are filled with risk and surprise.

The transformational paradigm transcends the rational planning process. It is concerned with deep change—with exploring new areas, tying new methodologies, and reaching new goals. The means to the desired end cannot be specified; they can only be learned as part of a risky, action-learning process.

To help convey a vision, a transformational leader will often engage in symbolic communication, creating vivid mental images for followers. These images provide a general guideline, as opposed to a specific directive.

Throughout the process of imparting a vision, the leader engages in unconventional behavior. The leader's actions are often beyond normal expectations and outside the rules of self-interest. For this reason, the transformational leader is difficult to understand. If the transactional paradigm comes from internalizing the organization, the transformational paradigm comes from transcending the organization. The transformational process involves a rebirth—a deep personal change—a hero's journey from which the leader emerges empowered and empowering.

Manifestations of the Transformational Paradigm

Lillian and Brubaker represent two very different worldviews. Both were managers and leaders in the sense that they exercised influence, as all managers do. However, Brubaker was a leader who held the transformational worldview. He understood the political and the transactional perspectives.

When leaders of deep change transform their organizations, they make a lasting difference. This usually requires a more complex understanding of the organization and its systems than the traditional transactional perspective. Lillian's transactional worldview is comprehensible. On the other hand, Brubaker's transformational worldview is difficult for most of us to understand. We see so many examples of Lillian and so few of Brubaker. Why?

Recall the engineer who transitioned from the paradigm of technical competence to the paradigm of political transaction. His realigned behavior patterns helped him shift into the new paradigm. When the technical paradigm led to frustrations, he was driven to a painful conversion.

In this sense, I believe organizations are natural incubators of the first two paradigms. Our educational systems and our career experiences in organizations naturally socialize us to the technical and transactional paradigms. The strategies of these paradigms are reinforced in nearly all our interactions.

Like the transactional paradigm, the transformational paradigm is reached through personal deep change. To internalize the transformational paradigm, the leader must become free of the organization's most powerful expectations, see it from a self-authorized perspective, and still care enough to be willing to be punished for doing whatever it takes to save the organization. Such processes are rare. Grasping the transformational paradigm involves personal change. Sometimes a person is required to leave the organization and operate alone, as is the case with many expatriates. Sometimes the process involves a career failure or a serious illness. In such situations, people often take the hero's journey. They empower themselves and learn to think outside the system. When they return, they see the system differently. They no longer feel dependent on the system and are willing to pursue what is right instead of what is acceptable.

The Transition to the Transformational Paradigm

Visionaries are internally driven leaders. They are able to appreciate but also see beyond technical competence and political exchange. They also exhibit an unusual characteristic—they do not view personal survival as a driving internal force. Their main objective is the realization of their vision. The leader and the vision are so integrated that if the vision lives, it matters not if the visionary should die or, in this case, be fired. Sacrifice of self for the good of the organization is an acceptable alternative. Identification with the organization is so complete that the leader is willing to die for the vision or principle because it is "right."

Few managers, including many CEOs, have internalized the transformational perspective. But the few people who have done so may be found at any level in an organization. These visionaries are known as transformational leaders and follow the moral-transformational paradigm. They may be generals, middle managers, or even high school teachers.

In internalizing the transformational paradigm, the leader becomes independent of the organization. The leader's behavior is self-determined and self-authorizing, and the leader is attached to the organization by choice, not fear. By taking a moral position and pursuing what is right for the collective, other organizational members are motivated by the leader's actions and power. They, too, are willing to take deep personal risks and follow their leader's direction because the leader believes in the vision, to the point that personal failure, firing, or assassination is acceptable. Thus when organizational members see their leader "walking the walk and talking the talk," they themselves are inspired to take significant risks for the good of the collective. The transformation of the organization progresses as the leader draws energy and vitality from this ultimate source of power.

Self-authorizing people are rare but dramatic. One extraordinary middle manager, who had served as an expatriate in two different developing countries (not an unusual background for people who transition to the transformational paradigm), returned to corporate headquarters and shortly began to challenge some of the company's most sacred doctrines. When told that his strategy was very risky, he replied, "If this company doesn't want someone like me, it doesn't deserve to have me." In this instance, normal logic is inverted. Notice where the actual power lies.

REFLECTION AND DISCUSSION

➤ Personal Steps to Change

1. List the key behaviors you expect from your leaders.

2. Given your list, do your expectations lie within the transactional or the transformational paradigm?

3. What elements of the transformational paradigm are the most troubling to you?

4. Describe someone you know who reflects the transformational paradigm.

5. Why are there so few transformational leaders?

6. What would make you more transformational?

➤ Organizational Steps to Change

1. Brubaker argues, "Every warden puts new paint on the walls, but the system stays the same." How does this statement apply to your group or unit?

2. To what degree is there a sense of vision in your work unit?

3. How could your boss apply the transformational paradigm?

4. How would people react if your boss applied the transformational paradigm?

5. List the reasons why there are not more transformational people in your organization.

6. What could be done to facilitate the development of transformational leaders in your organization?

Part IV

Vision, Risk, and
the Creation of Excellence

15

Overcoming Resistance

It is natural for organizations to discourage transformation. Organizational structures and processes encourage equilibrium, not change. In this final section of the book, we will consider the role of vision and risk in the process of unleashing power and achieving excellence. In this chapter, we will consider the untapped potential embodied in the middle management of large organizations.

The Pressures for Conformity

Neil Sendelbach is a gifted designer of executive education at Ford. For several years, he and I were jointly responsible for the creation and administration of the Ford–University of Michigan Leadership, Education, and Development Program (LEAD). This program was designed to transform the mind-sets of three thousand middle managers at Ford. We set out to help them initiate change in their organization and to empower them so that they would more effectively take leadership roles. This experience taught me a lot about the leadership potential of middle managers.

LEAD participants spent a week exploring leadership and change issues. At the end of the week, they were given a challenge. Each participant was to return to his or her organization; make an assessment of self, unit, and organization; and then institute a significant change. Six months after our initial session, the managers were to return and report on their change efforts. At our follow-up session, they were asked to identify the obstacles they encountered in introducing the change. A statistical analysis of their reports identified three major barriers (Spreitzer and Quinn, 1996). I believe that the same barriers tend to be found in most large organizations.

Three Barriers to Middle-Management Initiatives

Bureaucratic Culture

There are many ways in which bureaucratic culture proves to be a barrier to change, including multiple layers of hierarchy, a tradition of top-down change, short-term thinking, lack of top-management support for change, limited rewards, lack of vision, and an emphasis on the status quo. Several of these deserve comment.

In interviews, many of our participants mentioned the impact of a hierarchical management structure. One commented, "To get an initiative approved, five people must say yes. But to get it stopped, only one of the five has to say no." Congruent with this notion is the fact that in many organizations, there is a tradition of change from the top down. Initiatives for change are perceived to originate only from top management.

Participants also told us that change in their organization could be dangerous. "If you fail, you'll get punished." This was a commonly held belief. They also told us, however, "If you succeed, you may get punished." This latter statement surprised us and led us to further exploration.

Some people are "rewarded" for their success by being given additional work or by being seen as so indispensable to their unit that they cannot be promoted. Conversely, people can also be criticized or isolated by their peers or superiors. For example, in the blue-collar world, there is a well-known concept called the "rate buster phenomenon." This phenomenon describes a situation where one member of a work group generates more product than everyone else and is pressured to slow down. A lower work rate typically follows. This phenomenon can also occur in the white-collar world. The consequence is that people throughout the workplace are forced to think carefully about the "cost of success."

Our participants were also concerned about the absence of a vision. This complaint was directed at their individual work environment, not at the corporate level. Middle managers sometimes view their immediate bosses as politically oriented opportunists who convey no sense of commitment to any particular set of values. One day quality is sacred, the next day cost. If leadership means taking some risks and the values are always changing, how does a middle manager build a vision or direction for his or her own people? Working in such a confusing environment, it is difficult to know what to stand for.

Embedded Conflict

Conflict occurs at three levels. First, there is often conflict between functions in the organization. This makes it very difficult to take both a corporate and an innovative perspective in making change. Second, there is often conflict between peers who see themselves competing for the same position. This makes support for initiating a change problematic. Finally, many managers encounter conflict among their direct subordinates and are not sure how to address the problem. These types of situations make it difficult to proceed with any particular vision.

Personal Time Constraints

In today's world, people operate under intense time constraints. Increased work schedules and tight deadlines are pressures that middle managers face constantly. One may be doing a job that used to be done by two people. They often complain about having less and less time for family life. Working under these types of stressful conditions, middle managers often indicate that it is very difficult to think about initiating anything new.

The Three Barriers Taken Together

Bureaucratic culture, embedded conflict, and personal time constraints are barriers to change that exist within most large organizations. These pressures are not a result of bad intent; they are a natural consequence of the organizing process. Given these barriers, no matter what top management directs about the need to be empowered, the average organizational member receives a very clear message about what to do: Conform, don't rock the boat, choose peace and pay, and experience slow death (see Figure 15.1). The organization becomes a well-structured and natural "funeral parlor" for the ideals of initiative and leadership among middle managers. Middle managers receive powerful directives to conform from every aspect of their surrounding environment.

Middle Managers as Leaders

Given the strength of the barriers, can we ever expect middle managers to exhibit leadership in a large organization? The LEAD program taught us a lot about the answer to this question.

In designing the LEAD program, we assumed that we would find

Figure 15.1. The Pressures for Conformity.

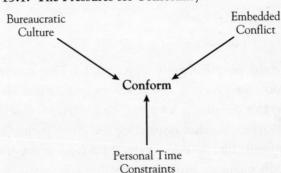

many barriers to middle-management initiatives. We concluded that these middle managers did not need new skills and competencies. In fact, they had complained that they already had skills and competencies that they were unable to use. What they actually needed was a new worldview, one that would help them act as empowered leaders in a changing organization.

During the program, we helped the participants assess the state of the world, the company, and their role as middle managers. We examined the tendency for an organization to strive toward maintaining equilibrium while at the same time inadvertently causing a slow death dilemma. We discussed at length the high costs of pursuing slow death. We pointed out that the CEO was never going to walk into the managers' office and wave a magic wand giving them more power. Empowerment is not granted by the organization. People must empower themselves.

Given the obstacles to change, reports in our follow-up sessions were rather astounding. Many participants succeeded in making deep change. For example, a loan-approval process at Ford Credit had been reduced to one week. After attending the program, one participant concluded that a week was not good enough, so she single-handedly took on the task of further reducing the approval time. Redefining her own position—electing not to do some of the things that were expected of her—she went ahead, at some risk, and successfully reduced the approval time to two days. Still not satisfied, she initiated another effort that resulted in another dramatic reduction.

Her story was not an exception. We heard hundreds of similar stories. In fact, there were so many such initiatives that the company decided to continue this very expensive program during a difficult financial time. For Ford, the return on investment was evident. In fact, so many significant changes were initiated and implemented that senior management labeled the program one of the company's best practices.

The Process of Personal Empowerment

In doing research on the experiences of the LEAD participants, we learned a lot about the cycle of empowerment. Attending the program provided a new kind of experience. It led participants to redefine their organizational roles and then to engage in new patterns of action. As one participant indicated, "The program forced me to reevaluate my core values, goals, and operating methods as they related to change. I made a conscious effort to become aware of my paradigms, and then I tried to expand my own and others' orientations to change."

The reinvention of self often brought innovative changes. When these managers were reinforced, they were much more likely to learn and to reflect on their new experiences. Typically, they felt more highly integrated with and committed to their organizations. The program expanded their perspective and encouraged them to explore new concepts and try new things. Many reported an increased sense of self-confidence and empowerment. Now they were willing to take more risks and test new ideas, often inspiring their subordinates to experiment with empowering behaviors.

Change means taking risks and facing the possibility of failure. Unfortunately, risk taking sometimes has a negative outcome. In the LEAD program, most of the initiatives were reinforced by the participants' superiors. However, approximately 3 percent of the participants reported being disciplined for taking initiative, and their anger was apparent. They told us, "Your program is a fraud. The company doesn't want leaders; it wants conformists." As can be seen on the right side of Figure 15.2, this process results in heightened feelings of disempowerment.

Overall, the participants indicated that they went through a process of redefining themselves and their organizational roles. They believe that the process began with deep thought and progressed into the development of a new perspective. Their enlightened state

Figure 15.2. Cycle of Empowerment.

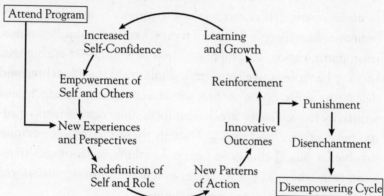

gave them the courage, the tools, and the empowerment to take risks and initiate action and ultimately the ability to incorporate it all into their learning process. The process is based on the continuous evaluation, reinvention, and realignment of self.

Types of Middle-Management Initiatives

In analyzing the efforts of the middle managers, we wondered what kinds of changes we could expect. Considerable data were gathered using both surveys and interviews. A statistical analysis of the survey data revealed that the participants made five types of changes (Spreitzer and Quinn, 1996). Let us take a closer look at each type.

Type 1: Management Style Changes

My initiative involved making major improvements in my personal leadership style. First, I worked to be more open and respectful of employee feedback and ideas. Second, I tried to achieve a better balance of coaching and criticism. Third, I attempted to pass responsibility downward by allowing my analysts to be the experts and defer to them.

The changes enacted in this category were typically alterations in management style or an increased sensitivity to the needs of subordinates. Most people described their efforts at building openness, trust, participation, and support. Their new mind-set encouraged them to be more active listeners and improved their coaching and delegating skills. Some of their initiatives suggested an increased sensitivity to such issues as customer focus, time management, quality, productivity, and safety. Though these changes sometimes involved a radical change in personal outlook, style, or sensitivity to an issue, they did not represent as much unit or organizational change as is seen in the other categories.

Type 2: First-Order Within-Unit Change

We needed to improve the productivity and efficiency in our department. Our previous attempts to introduce measurement systems had failed. Because of the varied and nonstandard nature of our workload, it was argued that measurement was not practical. I came up with a new method that measured total department test data rather than total worker-hours. I was able to get a trial implementation going. I presented the method and the trial results to the executive engineers and received enthusiastic approval.

The target of these initiatives tended to be the work group or department of which the middle manager was a member. Most initiatives involved well-reasoned attempts to improve things, such as cooperation, information sharing, planning, monitoring progress, productivity savings, safety, quality, and customer satisfaction. Methods frequently included instituting new meetings, reorganizing, changing a set of procedures, implementing new measures, or setting new priorities. These changes usually involved a concrete, well-understood problem, with little inherent ambiguity. Changes were more incremental improvements to the status quo, rather than radical changes that challenged basic assumptions.

Type 3: First-Order Organizational Change

The job of the database administrator (DBA) is to protect the database from errors caused by hardware or soft-
ware failure and to ensure efficient access to the data.
DBAs provide service to the data processing organization, which consists of application programmers. The
initiative was intended to get them to be more customer-
oriented. We undertook an initiative to increase responsiveness, but the early results were negative. We kept at
it and did a realignment between the DBAs and each of
the three application groups in the data processing organization. This greatly increased the customer focus and
improved our working relationships.

These changes are similar to the changes in Type 2 because they
are also attempts to resolve clearly defined problems. They are transactional or first-order changes. Type 3 initiatives used methods similar to those employed in Type 2, such as instituting meetings,
reorganizing, changing a set of procedures, implementing new measures, and setting new priorities. The primary difference between
Type 2 and Type 3 initiatives is that Type 3 initiatives are usually
aimed at the organization level. They transcend the boundaries of
the manager's group or unit. As a result, they are broader-based than
Type 2 initiatives.

Type 4: Second-Order Work Unit Change

We are responsible for three different computer systems
that provide divisional information. My department
consisted of three stand-alone sections. I reorganized it
into five "natural work groups." The five natural work
groups were set up around a customer focus. Instead of
being responsible for a specific computer system, as in
the past, the natural work group concept required all

team members to be concerned with common data, by vehicle, and to provide checks and balances on data across systems. The result has been more consistent and higher-quality data.

Like Type 2 initiatives, these changes tend to be targeted within a middle manager's unit or department. But unlike Type 2 initiatives, they are transformational or second-order deep changes. These changes may also involve a reorganization or a new strategy, technology, or practice, but they are much broader in scope and involve a reframing or reconceptualization of the status quo. In Type 4 changes, the problem that needs resolving is ambiguous. Consequently, basic assumptions about the way things are currently done are called into question.

To illustrate the differences between first- and second-order changes, consider the differences in the two computer-related examples given for Types 3 and 4. In the Type 4 example, the more second-order change, the more complex the change initiative; instead of simply reorganizing into different groups around the customer (as was the case with the Type 3 example), the nature of the task was also altered. The structure, relationships, and information were restructured to align groups according to the vehicle product they served. More so than the first-order changes (Types 2 and 3), descriptions of Type 4 initiatives typically included claims of high impact on the system and on the bottom line.

Type 5: Second-Order Organization-Reframing Change

At the end of the initial LEAD session, I made a commitment to substantially reduce product complexity on my vehicle lines. This would be accomplished by deleting low take-rate options, standardizing high take-rate options, and logically grouping other related options. Initially, I encountered considerable resistance. Then I got lucky in that there were some directives from the top to go in this direction. Now we have buy-in at all levels and across all functional areas. In fact, I'm now under pressure to speed up the process.

Like the Type 4 initiatives, these types of changes reflect the reframing of normal operating assumptions and involve an ambiguous problem. Also, these initiatives are more complex than the Type 4 initiatives, and their targets are different. Like Type 3 initiatives, Type 5 initiatives transect units or functions and sometimes the entire company. They also tend to involve many people. Examples of Type 5 initiatives include eliminating an entire process at a plant, a workforce reduction while increasing customer focus, a major reduction in conflict across two functions, and development of a new bid strategy that allows the company to reenter a lost market. Clearly these are second-order initiatives—system-level changes that involve the most risk.

Some Lessons from LEAD

Given the barriers to change that our participants faced, the variety and depth of their change initiatives was striking. Twelve percent were willing to engage in a transformational or second-order deep change effort at the unit level, and 34 percent of their efforts involved participation at the organizational level. First-order or incremental changes at the organizational level were reported by 16 percent of the participants, with 21 percent reporting efforts at the unit level. The remaining 17 percent reported changes in their management style. This suggests that, despite the pressures to conform, it is possible to stimulate and encourage middle managers to experiment with new patterns of behavior.

Paradigm Evolution

Although we learned many things from analyzing the results of the LEAD program, I would like to emphasize one particularly interesting point. It concerns the people who made the riskiest (Type 5) changes. Prior to attending the program, the participants had completed a questionnaire that evaluated their work environment and their lifestyles. On this instrument, the people who had initiated the Type 5 changes reported higher scores on health, job satisfaction, and personal relationships. Surprisingly, they were also the oldest group of participants. We believe that they had reached a career plateau yet had maintained a positive outlook. They were loyal to Ford and eager to make a significant contribution. Their perception of the "risk-reward ratio" was different. They were inclined to "do the right thing" because they were deeply loyal and less concerned with the "political risks" of making deep change. Whatever the reason, they had evolved from the political transactional paradigm to the more risk-oriented transformational paradigm. They were willing to confront the pressures of conformity and pay the price of deep change.

➤ Personal Steps to Change

1. Analyze the pressures for conformity in your life.

2. How do the pressures identified in Item 1 link with your sense of empowerment?

3. Given the model of the empowerment process in Figure 15.2, what actions would you need to take to more fully empower yourself?

➤ Organizational Steps to Change

1. "Bureaucratic culture, embedded conflict, and personal time constraints are barriers to change that exist within most large organizations. These pressures are not a result of bad intent; they are a natural consequence of the organizing process. Given these barriers, no matter what top management directs about the need to be empowered, the average person receives a very clear message about what to do: Conform, don't rock the boat, choose peace and pay, and experience slow death. Consequently, the organization becomes a well-structured and natural 'funeral parlor' for the ideals of initiative and leadership among middle managers." Assess the validity of this statement as a description of your organization.

2. Why do many leadership training programs fail?

3. If there is an empowerment strategy in your organization, how does it compare with the processes described in this chapter?

4. Outline a program that would help people in your organization feel more empowered.

16

From Manager to Leader

In talking with senior executives over the years, I have noticed that many have experienced the transformation from individual contributor to manager. They view their personal change as a significant life event. What I find most interesting, however, is that there is another possible transformation that most senior executives, including many CEOs, do not understand. That transformation is the shift from manager to leader.

Not long ago, I spent a day with a group of CEOs from a variety of midsize companies. As part of the day's activities, the group was asked to present a case study of organizational change. One man stepped forward and reviewed his tenure as CEO. He indicated that he had initially found it exhilarating to be in charge of the company. He described his early actions and how proud he was of his accomplishments. However, upon close inspection, he found the company's workforce lethargic and apathetic, exhibiting little initiative. After an agonizing analysis, the man decided that he himself was the problem. He had not been a leader but a manager. He needed to delegate his "management tasks" and begin tackling the larger long-term issues, including a cultural transformation within the organization. As he spoke, the audience nodded, clearly in agreement with the need for leadership in an organization.

However, when the presenter began to describe his risk-filled course of action, the audience grew uneasy. When he concluded, the audience immediately asked about the results obtained—a topic he had circumvented in his presentation. He displayed a graph that showed his company's performance indicators declining over a six-month period. The next graph showed an upward trend. His final graph demonstrated that the company was now performing at extraordinary levels. The session concluded with many of the CEOs expressing doubt and discomfort. They wanted to find an alternative explanation for the extraordinary success of the company. What this CEO had described was difficult to hear. It was almost as if they needed his story not to be true.

Though many people make the transition from individual contributor to manager, many, including CEOs, fail to make the even more difficult transition from manager to leader. Their failure to make the latter transition prevents many CEOs from recognizing their most potent lever for change and their ultimate source of power in the organization. The most potent lever for change is modeling the change process for other individuals. This requires that the people at the top themselves engage in the deep change process.

Leadership Behavior of CEOs

The tendency to deny and rationalize the need for the transformational paradigm raises a key question: Is transformational behavior of significant value to the collective enterprise? In a recent study of over nine hundred CEOs, Stuart Hart and I examined transactional and transformational behavior and how it related to the ability to enact deep change (Hart and Quinn, 1993).

We concluded that CEOs are expected to play four general competing roles: vision setter, motivator, analyzer, and taskmaster. These roles are part of a larger model (see Figure 16.1) encompassing four domains: the organization, the future, the operating system, and the market. Based on these domains, the model suggests four demands that all top managers must attend: the need for people, for innovation, for efficiency, and for performance. These lead to the four sets of expectations or competing roles.

Figure 16.1. Leadership: The Competing Roles.

Flexibility

Domain: The Organization	Domain: The Future
Demand: People	Demand: Innovation
Role: The Motivator	**Role: The Vision Setter**

Internal Focus ———————————————————— *External Focus*

Domain: The Operating System	Domain: The Market
Demand: Efficiency	Demand: Performance
Role: The Analyzer	**Role: The Taskmaster**

Stability

Transformational Roles

In the vision setter role, the CEO attends to the future, remains up-to-date with emerging trends, focuses on purpose and direction, and communicates a sense of where the company will be over the long term.

In the motivator role, the CEO attends to commitment, emphasizes company values, challenges people with new goals and aspirations, and creates a sense of excitement.

Transactional Roles

In the analyzer role, the CEO attends to efficiency of operations, evaluates proposed projects, and integrates conflicting perspectives and needs.

In the taskmaster role, the CEO attends to performance, focuses on results, solves problems, and influences lower-level decisions.

CEOs and Firm Performance

In terms of linking firm performance with the roles of CEOs, we measured three dimensions. The first was short-term financial performance as reflected in various accounting measures of current profitability. The second dimension, the growth and future positioning of the organization, includes measures of business performance, such as market share, sales growth, and new product development. In the third dimension, assessing organizational effectiveness, we looked at the nonfinancial aspects of performance, such as employee satisfaction, product quality, and social responsibility.

Our first question was, what roles are CEOs most likely to play? Before you read on, what is your prediction? Stop and order the four roles from the most to the least frequently played.

Our results may be surprising to you because CEOs are thought to be proactive leaders. We found that CEOs more frequently engage in transactional behaviors, like analyzing problems and driving task completion, than in transformational behaviors, like providing vision and motivating people. We found that the most frequently played role was that of taskmaster, followed by analyzer (both transactional roles). The motivator and vision setter roles (transformational roles) were less frequently played.

Next we examined the relationships between the roles and the three dimensions of firm performance. Though the taskmaster role is the most frequently played, it is unrelated to any of the three dimensions of firm performance. The analyzer role, however, is a significant predictor of business performance and organizational effectiveness, but it is not related to short-term financial performance. The vision setter role reflects the same relationships. The motivator role is related to all three dimensions of performance and is a particularly strong predictor of organizational effectiveness but is a weak predictor of short-term financial performance.

Given these results, we asked a final question: Do CEOs who perform all the roles get a different result from those who emphasize some roles at the expense of others? The answer is yes. The highest levels of performance are achieved by CEOs who frequently engage in all four competing roles. They achieve higher levels of performance regardless of the nature of their firm's size or the level of competitiveness in the firm's environment.

This study provided some insights into the uneasiness exhibited by the CEOs discussed earlier. For everyone, there is a natural attraction toward the controlling behaviors embedded in the transactional roles. These roles involve preserving the status quo. This attraction is highly consistent with the role of manager and the paradigm of political transaction.

In trying to lead, we face the challenge of overcoming the pull toward the transactional roles. This is difficult if we have not made the transition from the transactional to the transformational paradigm. In the transactional paradigm, we are more concerned about doing what is right for us than we are about doing what is right for the organization. We are more likely to be analyzers and taskmasters. Yet the key to being a successful leader is the ability to integrate and perform the roles of vision setter, motivator, analyzer and taskmaster. This requires the use of both the transformational and the transactional paradigms.

➤ Personal Steps to Change

1. Have you made the personal transformation from individual contributor to manager? If the answer is yes, describe the process. If the answer is no, indicate why not.

2. Have you made the personal transformation from manager to leader? If the answer is yes, describe the process. If the answer is no, indicate why not.

3. "The session concluded with many of the other CEOs expressing doubt and discomfort. They wanted to find an alternative explanation for the extraordinary success of the company. What this CEO had described was difficult to hear." Why was the message so difficult to hear? How might this observation apply to you?

4. In our research, CEOs frequently performed transactional roles, yet the highest levels of performance were achieved by CEOs with high scores in all four roles. What is your explanation of the findings?

5. We investigated corporate CEOs. Do our results apply elsewhere? What about middle managers, first-line supervisors, schoolteachers, or parents? How do our conclusions apply to your life?

6. The four roles are listed and defined below. Dividing 100 percentage points across the roles, indicate the percentage of time you spend in each role.

___ **Vision setter:** I attend to the future, remain up-to-date with emerging trends, focus on purpose and direction, and communicate a sense of where the organization will be over the long term.

___ **Motivator:** I attend to commitment, emphasize company values, challenge people with new goals and aspirations, and create a sense of excitement.

___ **Analyzer:** I attend to the efficiency of operations, evaluate proposed projects, and integrate conflicting perspectives and needs.

___ **Taskmaster:** I attend to performance, focus on results, solve problems, and influence lower-level decisions.

7. Given your estimates in Item 6, how would you like to reallocate the percentage points? How would you accomplish this?

➤ Organizational Steps to Change

1. How would you feel about working for the CEO in the first story in this chapter? Why?

2. What would happen in your organization if you began to initiate actions similar to the CEO in the first story?

3. In Item 6 in the Personal Steps to Change section, you assessed how you allocate your time on the four roles. Here you should indicate the percentage of time your boss spends on each role.

____ **Vision setter:** Attends to the future, remains up-to-date with emerging trends, focuses on purpose and direction, and communicates a sense of where the organization will be over the long term.

____ **Motivator:** Attends to commitment, emphasizes company values, challenges people with new goals and aspirations, and creates a sense of excitement.

____ **Analyzer:** Attends to efficiency of operations, evaluates proposed projects, and integrates conflicting perspectives and needs.

____ **Taskmaster:** Attends to performance, focuses on results, solves problems, and influences lower-level decisions.

4. How would you like your boss to allocate time to the four roles? Why?

5. What are the implications of your response to Item 5 for other leaders in your organization? How do they tend to allocate their time, and what is the impact?

6. How could you effectively make people aware of your insights on this issue?

17

Why Risk Is Necessary

There was a company that gave a critical product introduction assignment to a plant manager. The new product was a key element in the company's overall corporate strategy. It was imperative that the product be launched successfully.

The plant management team made an overall assessment of the project and discovered a problem. In exchange for cooperation, the local union demanded lifelong employment, a concept that was radical at the time. The local managers knew that if they called the corporate human resources division for permission, they would be turned down or extensively delayed by bureaucratic process. They also knew that if they proceeded without permission, they could be fired. After a painful review, they decided to meet the request of the local union and proceeded to do so.

The product launch was highly successful. Afterward, there was a follow-up meeting with a group of people from corporate headquarters. Initially, the meeting went very well. Then the proceedings turned to the role of the union. The senior executives were elated with the story that unfolded and discussed how the concept might be implemented elsewhere. Some of the second-level people were far less pleased.

This story illustrates an important dilemma. If the members of the plant management team had failed, they would very likely have lost their jobs for undermining the labor relations policy of the company. Yet if the launch had not taken place, the corporation would have suffered a significant strategic and financial setback.

Organizations need people to conform. Traditionally, rules and procedures have been established to ensure stability and pre-dictability in the organization. These rules and procedures are important, and a lot of time and effort is invested in ensuring their implementation. The rules bind the organization together and make coordination possible. Nevertheless, today's rules and procedures often represent solutions to yesterday's problems. The old rules often encumber an organization that tries to resolve new challenges from the external environment. To remain vital, an organization must adapt to its changing external demands. But this will happen only if a few people are willing to take a few serious risks. Organizational change always begins with a personal change.

Recall the revelation in the story in Chapter One that every transformational leader in the state government had broken at least one state law. This fact has a strange implication: to survive, orga-nizations need leaders who take risks and who care enough to die for the organization—which would kill them for caring. Most orga-nizations have few such people. When these leaders emerge, they usually have a vision, and their behavior reflects a transformational paradigm. They are self-authorizing and often follow unconven-tional methods that are based on moral principles rather than orga-nizational pressures.

If You Are Not Risking Your Job, You Are Not Doing Your Job

In Chapter Fifteen, I discussed the Ford–University of Michigan LEAD program. Initially, most of the participants were cynical about the objectives of the program. Many of their early comments were statements of skepticism and powerlessness like "Does my boss know what is being taught here? I can't do anything in this organi-zation. It is my boss who should be in this program, not me." The feelings of helplessness were gradually displaced as we explored an array of possibilities. As their attitudes gradually changed, they proposed a new theme: "Just do it," or JDI. This statement was posted on a sign for other groups who would go through the program.

During the early hours of each succeeding program, participants asked about the JDI sign. They often had a cynical response. A senior executive visited one such session. During the discussion with this executive, the newly arrived and still uncertain participants, seeking "permission" to be empowered, shared their cynicism about the JDI theme. They suggested that such an approach at Ford could be dangerous. The executive pondered this for a moment and then told a personal story.

As a young middle manager, he was notified by his boss that Henry Ford II wanted to expand a particular area of the business and that he was to complete the analytical work. He performed the analyses and came to a troublesome conclusion. His data suggested that the endeavor should be dropped altogether. He confided the details to his immediate boss and was told to "redo" the analyses. He repeated his work but arrived at the same conclusion. He returned to his boss and reiterated that if Mr. Ford proceeded with his plan, he would be making a mistake. At this point, a very unusual thing happened. Five layers of hierarchy cleared out of the way, and he was given the opportunity to make his presentation directly to Mr. Ford.

Ford was less than happy with the conclusions and asked the young man some very difficult questions. The young man was able to answer each one. Eventually, Mr. Ford announced that he was convinced, and the proposed expansion was canceled.

It is interesting to note that the man left the presentation without receiving any feedback. He had no idea if he had just destroyed his career. A few months later, he was transferred to Brazil. He spent the next several years wondering if he had been exiled. Many years later, he ran into someone at Ford headquarters who had been present at his presentation. The person told him, "You might be interested to know that after your presentation, Henry said, 'We need more young men like that one.'"

The executive reflected on his story for a moment and then said, "Every couple of years, you need to bet your job, or else you are not doing your job." His statement had a strong impact on the audience. He continued, "Yes, 'JDI' is correct. But you also have to remember something else." He walked to the sign that read "JDI" and wrote four more letters, "BDBS." He turned to the group and said, "*But don't be stupid.* You can't be wild, flying off on every issue. You have to pick the issues that really matter. When the good of the company is being sacrificed, then you have to take a stand."

Making a difference is important for both the individual and the organization. Though we often prefer to believe that nothing can be done about the awful problems we face, there comes a time when we have to take on the system because the system needs to change. There comes a time when we need to "just do it."

When we do decide to initiate action, there are no written guarantees, no insurance policies that will save us if we fail. The possibility of failure is a constant companion who walks beside every real leader. Leaders cope with this presence because they understand that whenever they sacrifice their principles for pressure, both they and the system take another step toward slow death. They are willing to accept the necessary risk because it is the right thing to do. They care enough to risk dying for the organization, which would kill them for caring.

➤ Personal Steps to Change

1. Consider the story about the man who confronted Henry Ford II. What did he gain or lose?

2. "Every couple of years, you need to bet your job, or else you are not doing your job." What does this statement mean?

3. Identify a time when you have bet your job or circumstances under which you might have bet your job.

4. What would be necessary for you to bet your job today?

5. What do your responses to the first four items tell you about your level of self-authorization? How would you like to be different?

➤ Organizational Steps to Change

1. "When we do decide to take action, there are no written guarantees, no insurance policies that will save us if we fail. The possibility of failure is a constant companion who walks beside every real leader." Identify a time when someone in your organization exhibited leadership and then experienced failure. What happened?

2. "Making a difference is important for both the individual and the organization. Though we often prefer to believe that nothing can be done about the awful problems we face, there comes a time when we have to take on the system because the system needs to change. There comes a time when we need to 'just do it.'" Identify a time in your organization when someone needed to "just do it" but no one did. Explain the situation and the outcome.

3. "To survive, organizations need leaders who take risks and who care enough to die for the organization—which would kill them for caring. Most organizations have few such people. When these leaders emerge, they usually have a vision, and their behavior reflects the transformational paradigm. They are self-authorizing and often follow unconventional methods that are based on moral principles rather than organizational pressures." Are such people needed in your organization? When? Where? What does your organization do to find or develop such leaders?

18

The Transformational Cycle

I t is common for the group of people who head an organization to refer to themselves as the top management team. I have worked with many such groups. Seldom has one of these groups actually functioned as a team. I define a team as an enthusiastic set of competent people who have clearly defined roles, associated in a common activity, working cohesively in trusting relationships, and exercising personal discipline and making individual sacrifices for the good of the team. When a team exhibits these characteristics, it performs at levels that exceed organizational expectations. The whole is greater than the sum of its parts. There is high-level cooperative interaction.

What I often encounter when working with top management "teams" is individual self-interest, anger, insecurity, distrust, little cohesion, and continuous political posturing. It is not unusual for the individual members of such a group to call on the rest of the organization to practice teamwork. Each individual on the top management "team" acts as if, and even overtly claims, that the top people are all "singing from the same songbook." No one in the organization dares to challenge the claim, but everyone knows that it is not true. Every display of self-interested political behavior on the part of management is noted and exaggerated as it passes along the "grapevine."

It does not take long for members of an organization to figure out when there is little cohesion within the top "team." This team is viewed by the rest of the organization as being insincere and lacking in integrity, and this perception breeds contempt at every level. As a result, there is little cooperation or sense of enthusiasm. In such a distrustful climate, people tend to their own self-interests. Political alignments and coalitions flourish. In this type of environment, teamwork is limited.

Since there are so many examples of groups and organizations that lack synergy, does it ever happen? Schlesinger, Eccles, and Gabarro (1983) quote an interesting statement by Dee Hock, former CEO of Visa International:

> In the field of group endeavor, you will see incredible events in which the group performs far beyond the sum of its individual talents. It happens in the symphony, in the ballet, in the theater, in sports, and equally in business. It is easy to recognize and impossible to define. It is a mystique. It cannot be achieved without immense effort, training, and cooperation, but effort, training, and cooperation alone rarely create it. Some groups reach it consistently. Few can sustain it. [p. 486]

There are several interesting points in Hock's statement. First, there are times when groups or organizations perform beyond our expectations. Second, however, this phenomenon requires immense effort and thus does not occur very often. Shifting from the current equilibrium or normal level of performance to a higher level means that a transformation must occur. At least one person must recognize that more is possible. Someone must then lead the group toward the collective goal. This transformational movement requires immense individual effort, communication, training, and cooperation, plus some luck. Finally, although some groups or organizations reach their goals consistently, this level of effort is difficult to sustain.

Bill Russell, once an all-star center for the Boston Celtics, helps illustrate the fragile nature of high performance. As a participant in one of the most successful dynasties in the history of basketball, he explains that on certain occasions, two opposing teams become joined in a synergistic relationship. This occurs when the outstanding effort of one team stimulates the opposing team to a higher level of play, which in turn stimulates the first team to an even higher level of play. At this point, the two opposing teams become a single, mutually reinforcing system. The impact on the individual participants is striking. Russell comments:

> At that special level, all sorts of odd things happened. The game would be in a white heat of competition, and yet somehow I wouldn't feel competitive—which is a miracle in itself. I'd be putting out the maximum effort, straining, and yet nothing could surprise me. It was almost as if we were playing in slow motion. During those spells I could almost sense how the next play would develop and where the next shot would be taken. Even before the other team brought the ball in bounds, I could feel it so keenly that I'd want to shout to my teammate, "It's coming there!"—except that I knew everything would change if I did. My premonitions would be consistently correct, and I always felt then that I not only knew all the Celtics by heart, but also all the opposing players, and that they all knew me. There have been many times in my career when I felt moved or joyful, but these were the moments when I had chills pulsing up and down my spine. [Russell and Branch, 1979, p. 177]

Russell believes that some individuals in professional basketball are gifted at encouraging their teammates to perform at higher levels. In his opinion, Oscar Robertson is perhaps the best example. Russell claims that Robertson could sense when it was time for his team to make a move. He would come down the court, stop at the top of the key, slam the ball into the floor, and yell at his teammates, pointing out that it was time to act. He would then fake his opponent one way, move the other, and sink a perfect jump shot. Russell comments that for the next three minutes, you had to really hold on, or your team would be blown off the floor.

From a leadership point of view, this analogy makes sense. A respected leader, with the information processing capacities of a master, senses when the moment is right and begins to raise the performance expectations of the group. Leaders are role models who support their colleagues in all their efforts, and they respond. However, if Robertson was so good, why did he not inspire his teammates to play at their peak level of performance for the entire game? Whenever I ask management teams this question, they inevitably laugh. It seems obvious to them that this expectation is unrealistic, that the human body cannot sustain such a high degree of intensity over a forty-minute period.

True, excellence cannot be sustained indefinitely. A few groups learn to reach it consistently, but they do not sustain it indefinitely. Excellence is a dynamic state, not part of a routine process. You maintain excellence for limited periods of time, and then you lose it. Furthermore, you do not reach peak levels by repeating exactly the same processes that worked in the past. Reaching a level of excellence involves analyzing each individual situation and determining what is right. It entails good communication, cooperation, high expectations, risk, and trust.

I shared these concepts with the top management team at an automobile plant. During the discussion that followed, one person confided that she could relate to one particularly important point. She briefly explained something that had happened nine months before. After intense effort, the plant had achieved new monthly highs on several key performance measures. Everyone was exhilarated, and every month for the next few months a new record was set. Then suddenly the numbers began to drop. The team members were trying to identify the reasons for the declines, without much success. My narrative had provided them with a new perspective. As a result, this team began to evaluate performance in a more dynamic and organic way.

Attaining Peak Performance

Most of us seek quantum leaps in our performance levels by following a strategy of incremental investment. This strategy simply does not work. The land of excellence is safely guarded from unworthy intruders. At the gates stand two fearsome sentries—risk and learning. The keys to entrance are faith and courage.

To attain excellence, an individual, group, or organization must care enough about an activity to insist that it fully meets and exceeds the demands of its audience (either internal or external), and this involves a fair amount of risk. Personal and organizational excellence demands experimentation, reflection, and evaluation, and these things in turn lead to learning and growth. Change precipitates growth—some part of the self or the organizational culture is abandoned, encouraging and allowing a new self or a new culture to emerge. The new self or culture usually leads to a synergistic relationship that results in high performance.

For example, a few years ago, Ford introduced a new quality evaluation program called Q1. Basically, it was supposed to stimulate deep change, and in many plants it was successful. To obtain a Q1 award, a plant had to pass an independent examination given by a group of hard-nosed outside evaluators. A Q1 rating meant that a plant had attained standards of quality that exceeded the performance levels found at most plants. Before the examination could take place, deep change had to occur throughout the organization. Consequently, almost everyone experimented with new processes and procedures. Plant managers took risks and then evaluated the results. They had to "build the bridge as they walked on it." They had to learn their way into a new state of being.

When a plant finally obtained the Q1 award, it was cause for great celebration. Leaders from the successful plant were often invited to speak to other groups and share their strategies and wisdom. I attended several of these sessions. There was a consistent flow of events at each one.

These presentations usually involved a person from an award-winning plant making a presentation recounting the plant's general history, the strategy followed, and the results obtained. The outcome was typically striking, and the audience would act suitably impressed. The discussion would then turn to the issue of greatest interest and importance for the audience: How does another plant achieve similar results? At this point, the presenter would typically become more ambiguous and begin to discuss such "soft" notions as experimentation and organizational learning. After a few minutes of this, someone in the audience would usually express frustration by saying something like, "Give me specifics. What do I need to do and when?" From that point forward, the discussion usually disintegrated.

After one such session, I asked the presenter about this pattern. He explained, "They just don't understand. They want a checklist, but this is not about checklists. This is about figuring out where you are and where you need to go and then launching an effort to get there. It's about learning. The key to becoming a Q1 plant is finding the unique strategy for your plant, for right now. Once you find it, you have to start looking for the next one, the one that will be right for tomorrow. There are no recipes. Why is that so hard to understand?"

Allow me to interpret. First we need to find a new perspective. Next we must start redefining the organization (or the self) by engaging the enactment process. During this process, we will gradually develop the unique map that will result in performance excellence at our organizations or in our lives. Why is this so hard to understand? It is hard to understand because it is close to heretical. Why? Because it suggests that organizations are dynamic. It proposes that leadership is associated with risk taking, learning, and change. It implies the embracing of uncertainty, the use of trust, and the exercise of faith. Words like these are not commonly found in the language of business. The language of business has a clear bias— toward equilibrium. To organize means to systematize, to order, to maintain equilibrium. Following this bias, managers are expected to routinize—they are not generally expected to explore risk, to learn, or to create. Nor are they expected to trust and cooperate, only to dominate and compete.

In actuality, both equilibrium and change are critical aspects of organizational life. An effective managerial leader must not only understand both but must also understand how to do them simultaneously. Such ability does not come from a list of hard-and-fast rules and procedures.

The Transformational Cycle

One key point that stands out in my observations is that excellence is a dynamic process. Every system of action is made up of subsystems. As subsystems, the Celtics and their opponents, for example, may become synergistic and reach extraordinary levels of performance, but this peak cannot be sustained because of the limitations of the other subsystems (the human bodies involved). An auto plant may experience quantum jumps in performance levels, but eventually these levels will also decline. The Ford managers who attained the Q1 award eventually arrived at the conclusion that deep change was necessary to maintain excellence and that risk taking and learning precipitate any transformation. People without such experience continue to ask for incremental checklists.

We need to understand that every system is continuously evolving. This evolutionary process can be described by the transformational cycle. This cycle has four distinct phases: initiation, uncertainty, transformation, and routinization. Excellence is something that happens as part of this cycle.

All action systems must expand and grow, or they will contract and fall into a state of decay. To remain healthy and vibrant, a system must continuously circulate through the transformational cycle. The system may be a marital relationship, a pickup basketball team, or a major organization. When the system keeps circulating through the various phases, it stays healthy.

However, it is not easy for a system to keep moving. There are four traps into which an individual or group may fall: illusion, panic, exhaustion, and stagnation. Each can lead to slow death—and in some cases a fast death (see Figure 18.1).

In the lower-right-hand corner of Figure 18.1 is the initiation phase of the transformational cycle. An iteration of the transformational cycle can be said to begin when, for whatever reason, an

Figure 18.1. The Transformational Cycle.

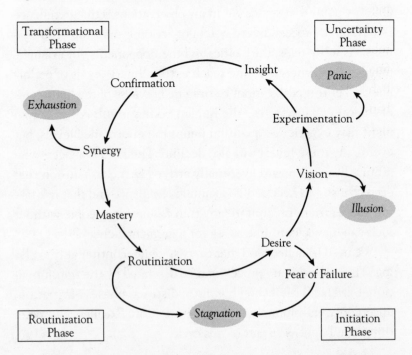

individual or group desires to change and improve. First, the person or group develops a vision and then begins to take risks. At the outset, it is often impossible to know if the vision is illusory or sound. A significant danger at this point is acting on a vision that cannot be implemented. If that situation arises, the person or group is caught in the trap of illusion or self-deception.

Despite an indefinite outcome, participants must progress from the initiation phase toward the uncertainty phase by engaging in intense, intuitive experimentation. If these action experiments continuously fail, the process could divert the individual or group from the cycle and into a state of panic. But if, instead, the participants are able to tolerate the resulting discomfort and frustration and continue to experiment, they may be able to gain a creative insight that guides them into the transformational phase. That is, through intuitive, experimental learning, the elements of the problem may be assembled or reframed, and a new theory or paradigm may emerge.

This transformational cycle is the essence of deep change. Having a new paradigm integrates the previously contradictory elements of the system and results in synergy. Relationships change. The rebellious teenager begins to communicate with the parent, who finally surrenders control; the desired partner responds to the new behavior of the suitor; the baseball player's new stance sends the batting average soaring; or the company's new product is consumed in large quantities.

In the transformational phase of the cycle, a person or collectivity could deviate from the cycle by entering a state of exhaustion. In contrast, the new vision, with resulting understanding, is routinized as the relationship moves into a more stable equilibrium or the task is fully mastered. Here again, a person or collectivity could depart from the cycle and fall into stagnation. Stagnation can lead to slow death. For deep change to continue, the transformational cycle must be complete. The change process will continue when there is an ongoing evaluation, reinvention, and realignment of self and the organization.

➤ Personal Steps to Change

1. Consider the description of synergy in the quote from Dee Hock. Make a list of the instances in your life in which you have had a similar experience.

2. Using your list from Item 1, what principles of synergy can you state clearly and confidently?

3. "Furthermore, you do not reach peak levels by repeating exactly the same processes that have worked in the past. Reaching a level of excellence involves analyzing each individual situation and determining what is right." How can this quote help you understand a problem in your life and begin to attack it in a different manner?

4. "Most of us seek quantum leaps in our performance levels by pursuing a strategy of incremental investment. This strategy simply does not work. The land of excellence is safely guarded from unworthy intruders. At the gates stand two fearsome sentries—risk and learning. The keys to entry are faith and courage." Apply this statement to a current problem in your life.

5. Using Figure 18.1, locate where you are in some important aspect of your life. Indicate the next appropriate steps you need to take.

➤ Organizational Steps to Change

1. Make a list of five teams that exist in your organization.

2. According to the definition of a team given at the beginning of this chapter, how many of the teams you listed for Item 1 actually function as a team?

3. "What I often experience when working with top management "teams" is individual self-interest, anger, insecurity, distrust, little cohesion, and continuous political posturing." Why is this sometimes the case?

4. List the reasons why an individual might have difficulty understanding the following statement. "They just don't understand. They want a checklist, but this is not about checklists. This is about figuring out where you are and where you need to go and then launching an effort to get there. It is about learning. The key to becoming a Q1 plant is finding the unique strategy for your plant, for right now. Once you find it, you have to start looking for the next one, the one that will be right for tomorrow. There are no recipes. Why is that so hard to understand?"

5. Identify a problem in your organization that fits some stage of Figure 18.1. How does the figure help you think about the next steps in the process?

19

Excellence Is a Form of Deviance

I once had a conversation with the CEO of a small company that had been acquired by one of largest corporations in the world. The small company was unusually profitable due, to a great extent, to its innovative and nonhierarchical management practices. At the time of the acquisition, the CEO of the smaller company emphasized the fact that the company's unique practices were the secret of its high performance and that the larger company might be tempted to alter the very thing that made the small company successful. The CEO was assured by the head of the larger company that this would not happen, and that if it did, he should feel empowered to resist.

Within months of the acquisition, the CEO's fears became reality. People from the larger company were continuously trying to intervene and instigate processes that would routinize the company's innovative practices. Countless discussions failed to divert the bureaucrats from their missions. Finally, the CEO simply called the heads of each staff function at the larger company and firmly informed them that if anyone from their staff showed up at his company, he would have them thrown off the premises.

His plan worked because he had the backing of the head of the larger company. The banished staff were furious, but there was nothing they could do. The man had taken a bold position that was supported by their boss.

A problem loomed on the horizon, however. The CEO was going to retire soon. His replacement was a highly qualified executive. I asked what would be likely to happen when the new CEO took over. He replied, "He is the person I would pick. He has most of the required skills and will do a good job. But he doesn't have what it takes to maintain my position. The people from the larger company will be relentless. They'll do everything they can to kill what is unique about this company."

This CEO was a leader who had successfully taken his organization through the transformational cycle. The company was striving to be on the cutting edge and was making the deep changes that led to excellence. Innovative behavior and unconventional methods differentiated the company from its competitors. Getting to such a point required vision, courage, and the discipline necessary to overcome resistance.

Resistance does not subside when a group reaches excellence. Excellence, by definition, requires continued deviance from the norm. When an individual or organization excels, it will encounter pressure to return to conventional behavior. In the case of the small-company CEO, the pressure came from the staff of the acquiring organization, but pressure could also come from other sources. Deviance will always generate external pressures to conform. To face up to such challenges and surmount them, an individual or group needs to be internally driven. Consider the following illustration.

"Because It's the Right Thing to Do"

While I was once making a presentation on empowerment, a man in the audience raised his hand and identified himself as being from a particular plant. I knew the plant well. Historically, it had been a place of poor performance and continual unrest. Everything about the place was bad. Then a complete turnaround took place. Management moved from the traditional assumptions of control and distrust to concepts of teamwork and cooperation. Nearly every practice and procedure shifted dramatically. After considerable effort and pain, the change paid off. The plant reached levels of performance that led not only the company but the industry. It became nationally known for its high-quality performance.

This man seemed very proud of the company's accomplishments and his role in the turnaround. This day, however, he appeared tired. He inquired, "How do you empower people when the corporation does everything it can to kill innovative efforts?" I asked him to explain. He argued that the company was not particularly interested in high performance and in fact did everything it could to discourage it. I asked him for an example, and he told the following story.

> Last week, we had a crisis on the shop floor. People from all over the plant willingly pitched in to confront and resolve the problem. Many people worked for over thirty hours straight. At one point, everyone was hungry, so the plant manager ordered pizza for everybody. The next week, I was sitting in the plant manager's office when the finance guy walked in. He threw down a piece of paper and said, "I'm not paying this." The plant manager picked up the piece of paper and became red-faced as he noted that it was the receipt for the pizza. He crushed it into a ball, handed it to the finance guy, and said, "You can do one of two things. You can pay this, or you can put it 'where the sun don't shine,' but I don't want to see it again."

He pointed out that this was just one of many small examples of corporate resistance to the innovative team approach. When he finished, I clarified his original question: "What you're telling me is that you have developed a highly innovative, highly successful plant that is very different from other plants in the corporation. You're regularly confronted by pressure to conform to rules and regulations that could cause you to become a very ordinary plant. The corporation keeps trying to wear you and your colleagues down, to make you ordinary, like the other plants."

He agreed that I understood the issue. I told him that I had an absolute answer to his problem—he should quit. I instructed him to return to the plant and tell his colleagues to stop trying, to give up. Give the company what it wants: become like the other plants.

He said that my advice was crazy. In reply, I asked him why he and his colleagues were trying so hard to maintain an excellent plant. He thought about it for a while. Finally he said, "Because it's the right thing to do."

I said, "You seem to be very proud of what you're doing. There appears to be a high level of satisfaction in achieving excellence. There also seems to be a great deal of pain involved. Every day, you meet some form of resistance, some force that would wear you down." He agreed.

I continued, "It seems to me that you have to be clear about something. Excellence is a form of deviance. If you perform beyond the norms, you disrupt all the existing control systems. Those systems will then alter and begin to work to routinize your efforts. That is, the systems will adjust and try to make you normal. The way to achieve and maintain excellence is to deviate from the norm. You become excellent because you are doing things normal people do not want to do. You become excellent by choosing a path that is risky and painful, a path that is not appealing to others. The question is, why would anyone ever want to do something painful?

"You have already answered this question. You do it because it's right and because it brings enormous internal satisfaction. That is the key. That's why I suggested that you consider giving up. If giving up becomes a serious option, it suggests that the external punishment is beginning to outweigh the internal satisfaction. We need to recognize that external punishment is a natural process that is never going to end. It forces us to weigh the trade-offs between internal satisfaction and external punishment. Usually this kind of contemplation supplies us with the strength to continue confronting the resistance."

When I finished, the man smiled and nodded his head. He had survived the original process of creating an excellent system. I had simply reminded him of something he already knew.

Lonely Is the Head That Wears the Crown

Sustaining excellence usually requires an internally driven leadership that is highly disciplined and not afraid of risk. When I was in college, I attended a talk on leadership given by Gordon Hinckley. At the time, my need for recognition made me very interested in leadership. I assumed that it was the way to obtain power. His talk, however, was not about the glory and drama of leadership. It was titled "Lonely Is the Head That Wears the Crown."

Mr. Hinckley passionately discussed the pain of having a great deal of responsibility. Few of us think about the pain suffered by those who dare to serve with both their heads and their hearts. This pain is considerable. The few times that I have become adventuresome and assimilated the transformational worldview, I have found the loneliness and pain of leadership nearly unbearable. Leadership is nothing like it appears to those who only follow.

Why, then, would anyone be willing to accept the pain that accompanies acts of transformational leadership? I suspect that such people have discovered that the pain of leadership is exceeded only by the pain of lost potential. They understand that excellence is punished, but they have developed a value system that provides no acceptable alternatives. They are internally driven leaders who are committed to continuing deep change and the pursuit of excellence.

➤ **Personal Steps to Change**

Write your interpretation of each of the following statements.

1. "Excellence is a form of deviance. If you perform beyond the norms, you disrupt all the existing control systems. Those systems will then alter and begin to work to routinize your efforts. That is, the systems will adjust to try to make you normal."

2. "The way to achieve and maintain excellence is to deviate from the norm. You become excellent because you are doing things normal people don't want to do. You become excellent by choosing a path that is risky and painful, a path that is not appealing to others."

3. "The question is, why would anyone ever want to do something painful? You have already answered this question. You do it because it's right and because it brings enormous internal satisfaction. That is the key."

4. "If giving up becomes a serious option, it suggests that the external punishment is beginning to outweigh the internal satisfaction. We need to recognize that external punishment is a natural process that is never going to end. It forces us to weigh the trade-offs between internal satisfaction and external punishment. Usually this kind of contemplation supplies us with the strength to continue confronting the resistance."

➤ **Organizational Steps to Change**

1. In the first story in this chapter, the CEO who was about to retire predicted that the unconventional behavior in his organization was going to get routinized. Identify an episode in your organization

when some unconventional behaviors that were leading to excellent outcomes were extinguished by the pressures for conformity. What happened?

2. Analyze the story about the excellent plant. Why were the employees feeling worn down by the corporation?

3. Analyze your job. Identify a situation where you were discouraged from engaging in the pursuit of excellence.

4. Identify the most important implication of this chapter for your organization. Prepare a memo, lesson, or speech that will make a difference.

20

Confronting the Undiscussable

Today, great emphasis is placed on responsiveness, cross-functional cooperation, and boundaryless organizational cultures. Yet these concepts fly in the face of centuries of hierarchical practice. For an organization to become a cohesive, top-performing entity, deep change has to take place.

The next section details an organizational intervention at a Fortune 500 company and the management commitment that facilitated the process. This particular top management team evolved through several levels of functioning. The process began with an analysis of the organization's present culture and the development of a new cultural profile and progressed to the identification of the specific personal behavioral changes that were needed to create the new culture. The trust and cohesion that resulted from everyone's commitment to the project allowed the team to transition to a higher level of operation.

Designing an Intervention

Traditionally, the business had been divided into a number of divisions, each of which offered the customer a different product or service. There were thick boundaries between the divisions, and each division head functioned as the head of his own kingdom. In a discussion of the company's future, the CEO and the general manager concluded that any customer should be able, without special effort, to access all the company's products and services. Since they wanted to present a seamless front to customers, they felt it was essential to have a top management team that really was a team. They wanted a high-performance team and a high-performance culture.

Though everyone in the organization claimed to agree with the new vision, little happened. Particularly troublesome were the division heads, who were used to operating in an independent manner. The general manager encountered continual resistance and, becoming increasingly frustrated, asked me to join him in trying to bring about a change.

After interviewing a number of people, I attended a two-day meeting of the management group. It was clear that these were bright, well-intentioned people who wanted to fulfill the organization's objectives. They were initiating a number of rational steps on the hard side of the change process. The tasks they were performing included rearranging boxes on the organizational chart and writing new policies. They were not, however, acting like a team.

Toward the end of the meeting, we discussed the team-building process and planned a two-and-a-half-day meeting to work on team building. We would begin by analyzing the culture of the team. We would then employ a series of exercises for analyzing and changing team members' actual behavior. We also planned a series of follow-up meetings designed to check on progress and to realign assignments, if necessary.

Diagnosing the Culture

The head of human resources, a man who was an experienced change agent, assisted me with the team-building meeting. On the first morning, the group appeared uneasy. We began with a fairly simple diagnostic exercise that analyzed the current and desired cultures in the organization. We used a technique that involved examining the competing values in the culture. (For an explanation of how to execute such a process, see Cameron and Quinn, 1997.)

The group consisted of fifteen people, representing both line and staff functions. In the beginning of the cultural analysis process, three subgroups of five people were set up. Each individual completed a personal analysis and then shared the results with the subgroup. Each subgroup compiled its results and shared them with the entire group. A comprehensive profile of these results appears in Figure 20.1.

Clarifying the Meaning of the Profile

The group found that creating the organization's cultural profile was an easy and insightful exercise. The results provided the material we needed for a discussion of where the company was and where it needed to go. After the discussion, I asked the participants to return to subgroups and carefully consider what was wanted in each quadrant. Subgroup discussion was structured around the following question: What does it mean—and what does it *not* mean—to increase, decrease, or stay the same in a quadrant? They were to list the important points in each quadrant. The results of this exercise are presented in Exhibit 20.1.

Focusing on Actual Behavior

The participants were pleased with their four lists. As a result, they were feeling very comfortable and confident. I indicated that this diagnostic process was consistent with their usual pattern of cognitive work and that we were now going to move slowly away from topics that were comfortable. We were going to zero in on their own behavior.

They were next asked to play a well-known simulation game called "Win As Much As You Can." Each person was required to contribute $20. Handing over their money seemed to increase interest. The game is based on the premise that if all the groups work together, they will all win money at the same rate. Eventually, the bank goes broke, and the teams have all the money. But the game

Figure 20.1. Organizational Profile.

The Clan Culture

An organization that focuses on internal maintenance with flexibility, concern for people, and sensitivity to customers.

A very friendly place to work where people share a lot of themselves. It is like an extended family. The leaders, or the head of the organization, are considered to be mentors and perhaps even parent figures. The organization is held together by loyalty or tradition. Commitment is high. The organization emphasizes the long-term benefit of human resources development and attaches great importance to cohesion and morale. Success is defined in terms of sensitivity to customers and concern for people. The organization places a premium on teamwork, participation, and consensus.

The Hierarchy Culture

An organization that focuses on internal maintenance with a need for stability and control.

A very formalized and structured place to work. Procedures govern what people do. The leaders prize themselves on being good coordinators and organizers who are efficiency-minded. Maintaining a smooth-running organization is most critical. Formal rules and policies hold the organization together. The long-term concern is on stability and performance with efficient, smooth operations. Success is defined in terms of dependable delivery, smooth scheduling, and low cost. The management of employees is concerned with secure employment and predictability.

The Adhocracy Culture

An organization that focuses on external positioning with a high degree of flexibility and individuality.

A dynamic, entrepreneurial, and creative place to work. People stick their necks out and take risks. The leaders are considered innovators and risk takers. The glue that holds the organization together is commitment to experimentation and innovation. The emphasis is on being on the leading edge. Readiness for change and meeting new challenges are important. The organization's long-term emphasis is on growth and acquiring new resources. Success means gaining unique and new products or services. Being a product or service leader is important. The organization encourages individual initiative and freedom.

The Market Culture

An organization that focuses on external positioning with a need for stability and control.

A results-oriented organization whose major concern is with getting the job done. People are competitive and goal-oriented. The leaders are hard drivers, producers, and competitors. They are tough and demanding. The glue that holds the organization together is an emphasis on winning. Reputation and success are common concerns. The long-term focus is on competitive actions and achievement of measurable goals and targets. Success is defined in terms of market share and penetration. Competitive pricing and market leadership are important. The organizational style is hard-driving competitiveness.

Exhibit 20.1. Meaning of the Desired Change.

Clan Culture
Increase means . . .
Meet employees' needs
Promote teamwork and participation
Support team players
Increase sensitivity
Better morale
High levels of trust
Concern for people
Self-management

Increase does not mean . . .
Becoming undisciplined and
   overly permissive
Cliques that jockey for power and
   control
One big "love-fest"
Only internal focus
Not working hard
Forgetting about goals
Protecting one another
   at the expense of achieving goals
Freedom without responsibility

Adhocracy Culture
Increase means . . .
Put dynamism back into the business
Create an environment where risk
   taking is safe
Encourage creative alternatives
Change as the rule, not the exception
Flexible and adaptive
Try new ideas
Forward-looking organization
Bolder innovation of programs

Increase does not mean . . .
Doing as one wishes
Running the business with reckless
   abandon
Disregard for customer requirements
Selfishness
Complete freedom
Missing goals
Dishonesty
The latest of everything
Taking unnecessary risks

Hierarchy Culture
Decrease means . . .
Eliminate useless rules and procedures
Eliminate unneeded reports
Loosen rules and structure
Reduce bureaucratic paperwork
Reduce corporate directives
Eliminate micromanagement
Remove unnecessary constraints
   Decrease does not mean . . .
Loss of logical structure
Inmates running the asylum
No rules
Letting people do their own thing
Elimination of structure
No production schedules
Throwing the baby out with the bath
   water
Taking advantage of the situation

Market Culture
Decrease means . . .
Slightly less measurement
Maintain commitment to winning
Quit driving toward numbers at all costs
Focus on key goals
Motivation of others
Adapt to market as well as human needs
Making money is still important
   Decrease does not mean . . .
Ignoring the competition
Losing our spirit and the will to win
Missing goals
Customer neglect
Missing profit
Stop looking at results

requires teamwork and, in actual execution, the groups usually take a competitive stance.

The participants assumed that "winning as much as you can" meant that their own individual group should have more than any other group. The game rules allow this course of action, but it requires posturing and deceptive communication between groups. Once this plan is initiated, a single group may dominate the other groups, but the bank tends to accumulate the most money. Within moments of the start of the game, the entire group was engaged in just such behavior. At the conclusion of the game, as is almost always the case, one group had deceived the other groups and won the "most" money.

In typical fashion, the "winning" group members waved their money in front of the "losers" and began to celebrate. As, also typically, the other groups became deadly serious and began expressing moral outrage. The winners were stunned and hurt. They quickly pointed out that the game was competitive and that winning was important. Their indignant opponents responded, "Either you live by principle or you don't."

This game generated conflict and, as a result, induced the entire group to consider some difficult issues about trust and cooperation. The discussion was exhausting. Afterward, we sent the participants outside to play volleyball. This was quite a departure from their normal work routine. These individuals would typically arrive somewhere in the world for a two-day meeting, begin work at 7:00 A.M. and continue until 10:30 P.M. The next day, they would repeat the process and then return home. They paid little attention to their natural flow of energy, their level of activity, or their exhaustion.

The next morning, I asked the participants their opinion of the simulation game. Most of the comments centered around the premise that once trust is violated, it is extremely difficult to restore. I asked the group what it meant to "win as much as you can." There were a variety of answers. I indicated my dissatisfaction with their responses by repeating the question. Gradually they realized that had they honestly cooperated with one another, the entire group would have had all the money and the bank would have gone broke. But they were still missing a vital point.

I asked them what they would have had besides the money. After a long pause, one person said, "Trust." I asked him to explain. He said, "We would have had the money, but we would also have had a tremendous sense of pride and trust among ourselves. That would have given us the capacity to perform at a level we have never really experienced before. I think that trust might be a greater financial asset than money. Trust is the means, and profit is the end. In pursuit of the golden egg, we often sacrifice the goose."

This was an important insight. People indicated that they had never considered an organization in that light. This led to an extensive and unusual discussion about cooperation and teamwork. They were beginning to see the value of trust.

Continuing, the participants were asked to list the times that they had taken part in a collective episode of high performance. They took their lists to their subgroups and identified the characteristics of a high-performance team. The subgroup lists were consolidated and written on a flip chart.

I revealed that to this point, we had just been warming up. Now we were going to tackle the real challenges, and some participants might not be up to them. I explained that these characteristics described a high-performance team and represented where they aspired to be. If they sincerely wanted to be a high-performance team, they would each have to make deep change.

They were given fourteen five-by-seven-inch cards. I explained a well-known intervention. On the front of each card, they were to write the name of one of the other fourteen people in the room. Below each name, they were to write the things they most appreciated and admired about the person. On the back of the card, they were to answer the following question: If we are to move from where we are today to become a high-performance team, what do I need from this person that I am not currently getting? (That is, how must this person change behavior if we are to become a high-performance team?) As a result, each person would receive fourteen cards with comments of appreciation and expectations for change.

The group was given an hour and a half to complete the exercise. The cards were then distributed to the corresponding participants, who were given forty-five minutes to read and analyze their cards and to prepare a response on what they had learned and what change commitments they were ready to make.

I indicated to the leader that it was his responsibility to respond first and that he needed to provide a role model for the entire group. If he ducked the pain of facing change, he would free the others to do the same. He stood up and reviewed the themes on his cards. He indicated what the group was asking of him and made some painful commitments that included performance measurements and follow-ups. It was a magnificent performance. One by one, everyone took a turn. It was a somber and reflective process. Several times, people were close to tears.

At the conclusion of the session, the participants were emotionally exhausted. They were sent to play volleyball again. Here a serendipitous event occurred. Their play was several levels higher than it had been the day before. The next morning, I shared this observation and asked why they thought their play had improved. After some contemplation, they indicated that their trust level was much higher. They felt more self-assured and had more confidence in themselves and their team members. They felt that these factors increased their ability to perform.

In the final session, we returned to our original task of planning cultural change. The participants identified and committed to specific programs and procedures that needed to be altered. Their plan came together quickly and reflected a consensus.

Two weeks later, I encountered one of the participants. He reflected, "In my whole career, I have never had a developmental experience that powerful. Several of us were recently on the corporate plane returning from Washington. You could tell that we weren't the same. The difference in our relationships is palpable."

Confronting the Undiscussable

The aforementioned session stimulated progress, which continued during our follow-up meetings. The participants wanted to keep moving forward and were ready to confront some of their real issues; they simply did not know how.

This group, like nearly all groups, had a problem with what Chris Argyris (1980, p. 51) calls "undiscussable issues." An undiscussable issue is one that is important to the group but is too threatening to discuss within the group. This group called its undiscussable issues "sacred cows." Group members believed that they were blocked by a number of sacred cows and really wanted to confront them.

During our first follow-up meeting, I asked them to reflect on their experience with undiscussable issues. They were to analyze what constituted an undiscussable issue and what the resulting consequences were. The following four questions and answers are a consolidation of their conclusions.

1. Why do undiscussable issues exist?

   Sometimes an undiscussable issue exists because of some historical events. When the issue first surfaced, tempers may have flared and personal attacks may have been made. The group probably sensed that it did not have the ability to confront the issue productively and so avoided it.

   Sometimes the issue never surfaces at all. One or more group members may send an implicit message that says, "This is an issue that must not be raised; if it is, I will be deeply hurt or uncontrollably angry."

   Sometimes an issue is an enormous threat from outside the company's culture. To evaluate it would be to consider something too painful for words. Denial is absolutely necessary. The group implicitly agrees to never consider the issue. Anyone who dares to raise the issue is, by definition, outside the group.

When such dynamics occur, people rationalize their actions so as not to confront and resolve the real issues. They argue that it is more painful to raise the issue than to live with it— there would be no successful resolution anyway.

2. What are the costs of undiscussable issues?

When undiscussable issues occur, people sense that the alignment between the ever-changing external reality and the internal mind-set of the group is beginning to decay.

Segmentation occurs at a number of levels and is usually reflected in the individual behaviors of group members. Their communication becomes segmented in that cognitive and emotional messages are not congruent. The exchange is intellectual, but with no emotional complement. People show no enthusiasm. They talk, but their words are empty. The value of the information that is exchanged drops. The process becomes inefficient. Time is spent, information is exchanged, but cohesive achievement does not occur. Value is not added.

Trust falls, and transaction costs go up. Only the easiest, most consensual decisions are made.

Innovation becomes unlikely.

People withdraw. The group further segments into coalitions, and backstage political action increases. At this point, trust and respect begin to decay.

People are categorized, and their behavior is often labeled with negative meaning.

Perceptions become self-fulfilling prophecies.

Harmful vicious cycles set in.

Individuals often have difficulty describing what is taking

place but clearly feel disempowered and helpless. The group moves toward a threatening situation with the individual members having little choice but to deny all the ongoing behavior that is driving them toward a crisis.

Groups generate the most energy when they are stretching and successfully negotiating the external challenges they face. Success is a function of creative congruence between internal and external realities. It is less likely to occur when there are significant undiscussable issues in the group.

3. Why do we not confront the undiscussable issues?

   A discussion would threaten the trust and cohesion of the group.

   Individuals fear that they would be unable to function effectively as a group if they processed an issue associated with such a high level of potential conflict.

   The potential discussion is often seen as a threat to one's self-esteem, credibility, and job security.

   Anticipation of such a discussion stimulates feelings of fear, anxiety, stress, tension, embarrassment, and pain.

4. What actions should a group take to deal with undiscussable issues?

   Obtain the help of a skilled facilitator and strive to emulate the facilitator's skills. Attempt to internalize these skills and implement them over time.

   Obtain individual perceptions of what the undiscussable issues might be. Submit these to a constructive framing and prioritizing process. Once the issues are identified, reengineer the group for each issue. Assess who needs to be a part of the discussion.

   Use the group's progress to build the working agenda. To build capability and trust, attack the easiest issues first.

Once discussion has begun on an issue, stay with it until closure has been reached.

Effective groups are simultaneously tough and supportive. They are dogged in confronting issues yet deeply caring and concerned about individual members.

Group members need to use supportive communication to facilitate cooperation.

Recognize that people are not likely to remain in the same position. Change, loss, and pain are necessary. People are willing to sacrifice self for the good of the group only if they believe in its purpose and health. They will often suffer a loss if they can be a part of an even more vitalized and successful group. They also need to believe in the sensitivity, fairness, and integrity of the central authority figures.

Realize that each confrontation is a new experience. The group must learn as it resolves the issue. Failure and pain are often part of the process. The group must understand that a short-term failure may be the beginning of the actual change process. Points of failure often require time for reflection, but the group must always return to the outstanding issues.

The measures of individual success should be congruent with the behaviors that are necessary for the success of the group. Technical competence, without loyalty to the larger group, is selfish. It is not competence at all. Some people will never be technically competent, and as a result, they may not be effective contributors to the group.

Individuals often experience an honest loss of some kind. When this occurs, it is important to help people recover.

Individual and group confidentiality needs to be carefully considered.

Moving Ahead

These observations provided us with a guide for moving ahead. We made a list of the group's actual undiscussable issues. There were ten such issues. After prioritizing these, we then began to confront them one by one. It took several meetings. There were many tense and uncomfortable moments, but we kept moving forward. By the end of the process, the group was at still a higher level of functioning.

This team is not perfect by any means, but it continues to grow. It continues to confront new issues and is adapting on all fronts. I doubt if anyone at the time of our first meeting could have imagined the present level of behavior. To reach this current level, team members had to work hard and make some difficult decisions. They all had to pay a price, a price that most management groups are not willing to pay. Deep change at the collective level requires deep change at the personal level. Organizational change cannot occur unless we accept the pain of personal change. These people did, and they grew into something more than they had been.

REFLECTION AND DISCUSSION

➤ Personal Steps to Change

1. What is an undiscussable issue?

2. Identify some undiscussable issues in a group that is important to you.

3. How do the issues you listed in Item 2 affect you?

4. What would it take to alter the impacts?

➤ Organizational Steps to Change

1. Review the process of cultural analysis. How could this process be used in your organization?

2. Analyze the index card exercise. How could you employ this type of process in your organization?

3. Identify and explain several undiscussable issues that exist in your work group.

4. Drawing on the ideas just presented, create a strategy for improving the ability of your work group to identify and confront undiscussable issues.

21

A Vision from Within

In meeting with middle managers in large organizations, the most frequent complaint I hear is, "I don't know what the vision is." I often tell the people to take out and read their laminated plastic card—the small document that spells out their company's vision, mission, and values. They shake their heads and say, "No, that's not it."

What is going on in this conversation? These people are telling me something very important, but what is it?

Today, much is said about the notion of vision. Though vision statements are now common in most large organizations, vision is not. Here we will consider the notion of vision and how it relates to the building of a high-performing organization.

Uncertainty and the Thirst for Vision

In the early 1990s, during a presidential campaign in the United States, a candidate by the name of David Duke emerged. His candidacy was particularly controversial because he had a history of being a racist and was a member of the Ku Klux Klan. I was deeply troubled, not only by his background, but also by the fact that there were people who were willing to follow him.

I grew up watching World War II movies. I coped with the devastation of the Nazi phenomenon by telling myself it was a

by-product reflecting Germany's turmoil in the 1930s. It was a historical accident and could never happen again. Yet the emergence
of David Duke demonstrated, in a small way, that it could.

Why is there always the potential for such a phenomenon? The
answer is not surprising. During turbulent times, people's uncertainty climbs, and they hunger for meaning and direction. They are
seeking someone who has a clear vision and communicates a clear
message. This knowledge should help us understand what middle
managers are telling us when they say they do not know their company's vision.

Uncertainty in Organizations

Not long ago, securing a position in a large corporation meant lifelong job security. This is no longer true. In today's world of hyperchange, organizations face more challenges and more uncertainty
than ever before. Organizational members often find themselves
feeling isolated, detached, and insecure. They crave a clear vision.
What they are actually encountering, however, is continuous
change and differentiation.

Because people want to know the company's vision, pressure on
top management to provide a vision keeps increasing. This pressure
often forces the top management team to sequester for several days
and engage in a "vision-finding" effort. After lengthy discussion and
negotiation over wording, the team comes out of the huddle and
distributes a plastic card bearing the vision statement. To support
this effort, everyone in the organization is asked to carry the card.

This process has value. I was present at an organizational gath-
ering of a Fortune 100 company when its retiring CEO was asked
to identify the most important accomplishment of his tenure. He
pulled out his plastic card and indicated that in generating the company's vision statement, he had accomplished more than in any
other act. His disbelieving audience asked him some hard questions
about his claim, but he stuck to his position and was relatively
convincing.

Generating a slogan to be inscribed on a plastic card is a valuable exercise, but it seldom satisfies the need that made the exercise necessary in the first place. Many senior executives are uncomfortable with the notion of creating and communicating a vision. They have difficulty coming up with anything that is persuasive, exciting, or passionate. There is no life in what they conceptualize. Worst of all, when they finally formulate a vision statement, it is not consistent with the behavior of the CEO or the top management team.

Who Is Willing to Die for the Vision?

The incongruity between vision and behavior is an important topic that is worthy of further consideration. I remember a visit I made to a large company. A task force composed of the company's top executives had been given three months to generate a vision statement. I met with the members of this group and read the nearly completed statement.

After a lively discussion about their product, I asked, "Who is willing to die for this vision?" No one spoke up. My question had surprised them and made them somewhat uncomfortable. Why? Because as a politically segmented group, they had executed a rational exercise and forged some abstract generalities into a statement to which no one could object. However, whether undertaken by an individual or a group, a worthwhile vision does not come from painless compromise.

Statements that emerge from such efforts are empty words. They are not inspiring because they are not visionary. Statements that are not motivating do not encourage people to change their behavior. No one "talks the talk" because the talk is meaningless.

Developing a vision is a very difficult and tortuous process because it requires something more than a superficial analysis. It involves confronting the lack of integrity that exists in the system. Few people are equipped for such an exercise. That is why most vision statements are empty and why most people feel there is no vision in their organization. When people express their yearning for a useful vision, it irritates the company leaders, who typically feel inadequate about their inability to provide that vision.

Tell Them to Stop Saying That

Many senior people have no idea how to develop a vision and find it very embarrassing to be reminded repeatedly that their company lacks an adequate vision. As a consequence, it becomes necessary to stop talking about the needs they are not meeting. They implicitly send the message that the issue is no longer discussable.

However, sometimes the situation warrants a message that is more explicit. I know one executive who heard middle managers continuously claim that they did not know the company vision. Finally, he met with his top management team, and together they generated a plastic card. Sadly, within a week, the message circulated again, "We don't know the vision." Finally, in frustration, he turned to one of his vice presidents and said, "Go tell them to stop saying that."

People often laugh when I tell this story. I repeat it, not in derision, but with empathy. I have tried to convey a vision to others. It was a frustrating experience. It is much easier to focus on solving today's problems than it is to mold the future. It is easier to be an operational analyzer and taskmaster than it is to be a developmental and visionary motivator.

Yet transformational leaders can do both. They link the operational present with the developmental future. That is what makes them persuasive. Useful visions inspire people to new levels.

On Finding Bread and Salt

When I encounter the yearning for vision in a organization, it often leads to a discussion with the senior leaders. Frustrated, they show me their official vision documents and ask me why they are not effective. Sometimes I respond by saying that their documents do not reflect bread and salt. I then share with them a story from the movie *Gandhi*.

In the early part of his career, Mohandas Gandhi successfully confronted some forms of discrimination in South Africa. When his work was completed, he returned home to India. Gandhi was encouraged to become involved in politics. Instead, he went on a long journey through his homeland. His travels led him through the countryside, where he visited many villages and farms. Gandhi endured many unpleasant conditions as he patiently listened to the peasants and observed their surroundings.

Shortly thereafter, a political convention was held. The country's top politicians attended and gave rousing speeches calling for home rule and expulsion of the British. The audience was largely in agreement and loudly expressed support. Finally, the unpretentious Gandhi was given a chance to speak. When he was introduced, people left their seats and began to wander around the convention floor.

Gandhi began his low-key speech by talking about the "real" India. India, he argued, was not about home rule. The citizens of India did not really care who was ruling the country. What they did care about was bread and salt. Unless the politicians understood the issues of bread and salt, which they did not, the voters would simply be replacing British tyrants with Indian tyrants.

As Gandhi continued speaking, people gradually returned to their seats and began to listen. Why? Because they were hearing something unusual, something of great importance. This small, unassuming man had journeyed through their heartland and captured the essence of India. He was now vocalizing it in a way they could feel and understand. Such articulation is often at the heart of radical, deep change.

The term *radical* is derived from the Latin word for "root." In mathematics, for example, we use the radical sign to indicate the square root. To make radical change, one must move to the root, the origin or archetype. An influential vision reflects the insight of an individual or group that has deeply contemplated the core issues. Gandhi's vision was such a reflection. It was rooted in both facts and values. It inspired passion.

A visionary leader delves into the core of the organization or group and touches the issues of bread and salt. Few senior executives ever do so. They are thus greatly hindered in the process of aligning the operational present with the developmental future.

It is sometimes difficult to touch the issues of bread and salt because of the upward filtering process in the organization. Almost every message an executive receives from subordinates is finely filtered and highly polished. In a hierarchy, we seldom really know what is going on below us. Sometimes we are uncomfortable being around "the masses." I remember hearing stories about particular auto executives who could not stand to be in meetings with the "slimy" auto dealers. Similar snobbishness exists in most large organizations.

Isolated and insulated people cannot succeed at motivating others. When they finally generate a vision document, its message will be frail and uninspirational. Usually the "walk" of such people will not match their "talk," and the real message is clear. Nothing happens, and the vision document soon slides into decay and obsolescence.

A CEO Finds a Vision

Is it realistic to expect an executive in today's world to get in touch with the issues of bread and salt? It is not only realistic but essential. It is therefore helpful to consider a case when it did occur.

One large company I am familiar with had a long record of financial success. Suddenly, the world changed, and the company faced extreme financial difficulty. Everything that had made it successful was now in question. It found itself in the midst of a crisis, and people were frustrated. They were looking for a new vision from their new CEO. But despite a great personal effort, the CEO declared that he had no new vision statement.

In light of the deteriorating situation, the company's top management decided that an immediate intervention was necessary. Several well-known professors were brought in to design a program. There would be a series of four one-week meetings. Each meeting would be held with one hundred of the company's top executives— four hundred in all.

Our top priority was to see that this company confronted and resolved real issues. Yet in this company, there was seldom any kind of public conflict. This made the design of our intervention difficult.

The proposed intervention would begin with introductory presentations on finance and strategy. Next I was to direct a session designed to move toward the identification and analysis of the other issues the organization faced. In preparation for my part of the program and to understand the culture of the company better, it was suggested that I interview some of the people who would attend the session.

I conducted the interviews and subsequently found myself putting my insights in writing. Portions of the resulting document follow.

The Inner Voice of the Organization

During our life, we often experience periods when we seem to lose our sense of meaning. There is no longer a feeling of alignment between our inner values and our external tasks. We find ourselves working harder and harder and receiving less satisfaction from our efforts. We struggle through every day, lacking the vitality, commitment, and initiative we used to have. After much inner reflection and contemplation, we begin to realize that we need a new focus, a new vision, but it is difficult to uncover. By way of illustration, consider the following story.

I have a young friend whose life was in great turmoil. She was intensely focused on the accomplishment of a few key tasks. Her intensity was often a source of difficulty. She frequently found herself at odds with both her family and her employer. Her confrontations with these people escalated until she reached a state of continuous, intense anger. Her productivity declined, and she sensed that she was becoming less functional.

One day, instead of going to work, she went for a hike on a nearby mountain. After several hours of climbing, she reached the peak. Exhausted, she sat down to rest. She was there only a few moments when she realized she was not alone. Three people stood nearby preparing to hang-glide. One by one, they pushed off the edge and leapt into the wind currents. She watched as they gradually descended to the floor of the valley. When they landed, she could barely see them.

This overview caused her to do a great deal of inner reflection that had a great impact on her future. She thought about her own conflicts and how insignificant they were in the scheme of life. She wondered if perhaps she had lost her perspective. As she stood there, she concluded that her confrontations were more destructive to herself than to others. This insight was particularly potent, and she resolved to confront her problems in a different way. She returned home with a new outlook and a sense of relief. She believed that from that day forward, her life had turned around.

The interesting thing about this story is that my friend's resources for change were all internal. Her stimulation came from viewing the vast panorama, but the actual resolution to her dilemma was already embedded within her. Her inner voice was telling her that she was not acting productively and that her actions were becoming self-destructive. Her inner voice led her to extricate herself from the logic of task pursuit. It led her to climb a mountain—to put herself in a position where she could clearly hear her inner voice. After viewing the vast panorama, she began to take on a larger perspective of her surrounding environment. She could, for the first time, confront the reality that she had been denying— that her coping strategies were failing. She realized she could not survive and thrive unless she did things in her life differently. She needed to adjust the alignment between her inner values and her external realities.

Listening to the Inner Voice of the Organization

An organization also has an inner voice. Like the individual inner voice, it also calls for the continuous realignment of internal values and external realities. Since a realignment usually implies some kind of deep change, the inner voice is an enemy to the existing insecure organizational culture. This culture needs to preserve itself, so it works to silence the inner voice, and it is usually effective. What nearly everyone knows individually cannot be voiced collectively.

Unlike the inner voice of the organization, the individual voice always maintains a self-interest. The organizational voice, in contrast, wants the organization to succeed. So the organizational voice bows to truth and pays little homage to power. It seeks to expose painful realities. In seeking the collective good, the inner voice does not distort the needs for sacrifice and change by deferring to the preferences of a particular individual. The inner voice of the organization is often a threat to those in authority.

Interestingly, the inner voice is the most potent source of power in the organization. The inner voice leads to realignment and an increased flow of resources. The inner voice finds root in the moral core of the organization. When individual effort disconnects from the inner voice, people begin to lose vitality. Energy is lost. Human commitment begins to decay.

Discovering the inner voice of the organization helps uncover a vision filled with resonance. To accomplish this task, an individual or a group must be willing to break the logic of task pursuit. Preparation, reflection, and courage are necessary in order to hear the inner voice. The inner voice will provide direction if people have the courage to listen and the commitment to change.

The purpose of the document featured in the following section was to articulate the inner voice of this company. It is the result of interviewing members of the organization. It is an integration of the messages in the hearts and minds of many. That is where the organizational inner voice resides. As an outside interviewer, I honored the collective inner voice by the simple act of listening. By paying attention to the themes running across the interviews, I uncovered an underlying structure. What follows is not the voice of any one person but the collective voice residing in the shadows of each individual. It represents the inner voice of the organization.

An Interview with the Inner Voice of the Organization

The original document contained eight questions and answers. Each answer described a key issue facing the company and was illustrated by a concrete example. Each concerned an undiscussable issue. Each such issue represented a weakness or a need within the company. They are summarized as follows:

- The company is characterized by loyalty and considerable unused human potential.

- The organization must make deep change in order to become more viable and thus be able to survive in a rapidly evolving world.

- The company is hampered by an unconscious conspiracy of silence and an inability to confront issues and identify needed adjustments.

- "Groupthink" is widespread, and models for constructive conflict are lacking.

- Certain key figures have favored individual good and self-interest over the collective good, and they have been reinforced.

- Everyone would like to believe that certain transparent issues are successfully kept secret. Individuals try to save face by pretending that no one knows what everyone knows—and the process works as long as no one listens to the organization's inner voice.

- A cohesive leadership team is lacking.

- The company has no clear, believable, and motivating vision.

Summary and Implications for Action

The document's summary statement reads as follows:

The inner voice has spoken. It articulated eight important issues keeping this organization from moving forward. Surprisingly, while the inner voice spoke frankly about the top of the organization, it did not place the responsibility for these problems on the top management group. The inner voice is a mature voice, and it sees the system as a system. It recognizes that the responsibility for deep change does not belong only at the top but with every individual. It recognizes that every individual is really the CEO. The problem is that the hierarchical culture will not tolerate this truth, and terrified individuals rationalize it away and project responsibility on the authority figures.

As always, the voice has spoken frankly. What does all this mean, at this point, in this conference? We have analyzed the company strategically and financially. We have listened to the inner voice. What is required of us now?

At this very moment, we decide if we dare to reinvent the culture. It is a critical moment that few companies ever confront. Most companies are not healthy enough to get this far. They are too sick to be healed.

In the next few days, and beginning with this moment, we have to decide if we dare to have a company that lets truth speak to power. We must decide if we dare to have constructive conflict. If asked overtly, we all, by necessity of social desirability, answer yes. We want to hear and speak the truth. But with our body language and our behavior, we send the screeching message that we do not want to hear any message that suggests any need for sacrifice or change on our part. Nor do we want to take foolish risks with those in authority. Whenever we look up the system, we understand this perfectly. We have all mastered the art of looking for the raising of the eyebrow, the shift in weight, or some other cue that tells us we are getting too close to some zone of discomfort.

Looking down the system, we see no such behavior on our own part. We tell our subordinates that the door is always open. We tell them that they should be empowered. Occasionally, they make the mistake of taking us seriously and act on their own. For a moment, they become responsible adults. Their act of independence makes us uncomfortable, and we let them know how we really feel. They respond in amazement, "Oh, that is what you meant by empowerment. Now I understand. You don't need to worry anymore."

When we read these words, we must all make the decision that we would like the CEO to make. We want our boss to become emotionally engaged, to bring charisma into our lives, to reduce our ambiguity and point us safely into the promised land. However, the real questions are, Do I care enough to do that myself? Am I courageous enough in my senior roles to listen, to give subordinates permission to ask about my contribution to existing difficulties? Am I brave enough to ask myself if I am choosing slow death for the corporation? Can I recognize when it is time to leave? In my subordinate roles, am I courageous enough to be the CEO? Am I willing to take charge of the company by assertively pursuing the collective good, even if I have to enter the danger zone of a senior person? That is, am I willing to take real risks for the good of the company?

These are the real questions upon which the future of the company pivots. They will be answered in the next few hours and the next few days. Today, we begin to climb our own organizational mountain. We will see the panorama, we will examine our past, we will look at ourselves. By the end of the week, we will know, as the inner voice knows, where the company has been, where it is, and where it dares to go.

Designing the Intervention

I sent the original document to the CEO and explained that I thought it would be a very useful tool to introduce at the outset of the program. I suggested the following design. After a short introductory presentation, the document would be distributed to each of the one hundred participants. They would be asked to identify what they considered the five most important points in the document. They would then be divided into small subgroups and asked to identify its five most important points. We would then integrate the lists from the subgroups and establish the key issues. This design would allow the group to discuss the undiscussable issues honestly and provide an action agenda for the week.

I expected the CEO to reject my plan. Instead, he made a few factual clarifications and then indicated that if it would help get the job done, the document should be used. I was impressed. In similar situations I have encountered, many executives shy away from any confrontation with the real issues.

Finding a Vision

Using the document fulfilled our original objective of opening an honest dialogue. The CEO attended the first week. We advised him to listen to everything but to say very little, even when he knew that certain statements were not factual. It was a time for others to speak and feel safe. He needed to listen.

During the week, the exchange of ideas and opinions was intense and constructive. My colleagues motivated and encouraged the participants to speak candidly. For the first few days, the CEO was blamed for nearly every problem. Gradually, however, the tone of the sessions began to change. People began to look closely at themselves and to assume some responsibility for the organization's undiscussable issues. Close to the end of the program, we discussed several of the remaining issues. I then turned to the last paragraph of the document:

> These are the real questions upon which the future of the company pivots. They will be answered in the next few hours and the next few days. Today, we begin to climb our own organizational mountain. We will see the

panorama, we will examine our past, we will look at ourselves. By the end of the week, we will know, as the inner voice knows, where the company has been, where it is, and where it dares to go.

At the beginning of the week, the executives had been demanding that the CEO provide them with the great integrating vision—that he should stand up and tell them exactly what to do. Now, I pointed out, they knew the vision. No one had vocalized it, but it existed within them. They had all the information and tools that were necessary.

I asked the participants to rewrite the document concerning the company's inner voice. They needed to identify what the inner voice of the organization was now saying to them individually. They were to consider a vision and a strategy for their own stewardship and share it with their subgroup. This exercise proved to be an enlightening and rewarding experience for many. Most of the participants discovered that they really did have a sense of direction for themselves and their organization.

The final session was a speech by the CEO. He spoke for an extended period with unusual candor and passion. At the conclusion, he was given a standing ovation. One individual walked up to the CEO and hugged him, an act symbolic of what most were feeling. As he left, another senior person said, "I would walk through a wall for that man. I'm going home, and I know exactly what I need to do."

Subsequently, the CEO made an interesting decision. He cleared his calendar and allocated three weeks to attending the three remaining "follow-up" sessions. Why would he make such an extraordinary commitment? Because he was getting in touch with the core of the organization.

Interestingly, he presented his "vision" at the third one-week session. He now knew what the company needed to do. The new vision was very specific, and it required enormous sacrifice by various groups in the company. It was accepted with enthusiasm and commitment. He had discovered bread and salt.

In the months that followed, deep changes occurred at many levels in the company. There was enormous progress and tremendous political conflict. Many people suffered, including those at the top. However, they were slowly resolving their undiscussable issues, and the organization began to move forward.

Building Commitment Without a Bread-and-Salt Vision

It is not unusual for someone to ask me where a vision should come from and how the vision should be communicated. Should the process be from the bottom up or from the top down? Usually the questioner has a strong opinion about one perspective or the other and is not really asking a question at all. Those who believe it should come from the top down think that the leader should find a vision and implement it. Those that hold the bottom-up perspective feel that there should be an inductive process of discovery in which participation is used to engender ownership.

In the story about finding a bread-and-salt vision, a circular process was taking place. The bottom-up process provided the CEO with the input he needed to develop his own vision, which he implemented from the top down. It was his own vision, yet it clearly took root from the frank expressions of his subordinates. He was involved in an important dialogue. Because he touched the core of the system, the system readily accepted his vision.

The circular process tends to occur even with the most strong-willed individualists. For a marvelous example of such a person, watch the movie *Patton*. General Patton appears to be the ultimate self-willed leader. Yet he is constantly communicating with his men. It is difficult to see beyond his domineering personality, but he is subtly gaining input. Even Patton learned from the bottom up. He was clearly capable, despite his authoritarian personality, of touching the bread-and-salt issues.

The Power of Dialogue

A fine case study and video have been generated by the Harvard Business School, about a change process that occurred at Johnson & Johnson. J&J had something called the Credo. It was the company's statement of values and operating principles, and it had been used for many years. J&J is a global organization; in some parts of the world, people paid attention to it; others ignored it or had never heard of it.

The CEO decided that the Credo needed to come alive or be killed. He traveled all over the world, holding meetings to discuss the document. The meetings were held after working hours but were well attended, and opinions were intensely expressed. As a result, he revised the document. Many wondered if this was a wise allocation of his time.

A short time later, J&J had to deal with the widely reported Tylenol crisis. Poison was inserted into a few Tylenol bottles with life-threatening consequences for consumers. Analysts argued that the product was dead.

Later, in reflecting on the crisis, the CEO indicated that in such times, numerous decisions must be made simultaneously in all parts of the world. There is no way to manage such a crisis. He could only trust the corporate value system and hope that everyone did the right thing. Most people did. In fact, the crisis was so well managed that the product survived. In recapping the story, the CEO noted that the worldwide discussions had helped clarify the company's values in the minds of its people. He stated that there was now a common mindset at all levels in the company. His bottom-up effort, plus an unforeseen event, had created a commonly shared vision.

I know of another company that had a vision document that was having little impact. Someone came up with a radical proposal to resolve the problem: hold a contest. Everyone in the company was issued a child's wooden block. Each block had to be combined with the blocks of others within a common work group. The combination of blocks had to represent some part of the vision statement.

Many people participated in the contest, and the prizes that were awarded were significant. The entries demonstrated extreme creativity. Groups assembled beautiful objects representing value statements in the document. One group, for example, focused on diversity. Group members turned their blocks into sawdust, made masks of the various faces represented in the company, melded them into a single sculpture, and painted it. Another group focused on cross-functional cooperation and built a beautiful bridge.

The winning entries were announced at a large celebration. This was an extraordinary event and well outside the company's cultural norm. The cultural environment reaped great rewards from the contest. The contest brought the vision to life. It became a guide for action.

Vision from Discipline

In a less creative and more disciplined approach, one company with a seemingly dead document brought it to life by using a rigorous policy. Every company meeting had to begin and end with a review of the document. However, this was not a welcomed policy. No one wanted to do it. The policy was enforced at the absolute insistence of a strong authority figure. Eventually, the endless discussions brought the vision to life and resulted in changed behavior.

I know of still another case in which a noncharismatic, almost painfully shy man took over an organization. He exhibited few of the classic characteristics of transformational leadership. What he did have, however, was an intense financial discipline. He established a very clear strategy to which few initially paid attention. Virtually every request that did not clearly relate to the strategy was denied. This caused considerable conflict, but people began to pay attention. He set off a top-down process that would eventually bring new direction. The new direction created a sense of possibility in the lower ranks, and people began to come forward with creative proposals that were consistent with the new direction. A deep change followed.

No one would describe this man as a visionary leader. He himself chokes on the word *vision*. Yet I would argue that this man is both visionary and transformational. His visionary process was both top-down and bottom-up. The top-down process is obvious. What is less obvious is that during all the conflicts, he was continually learning, and like Patton, he was finding out the core needs of his organization. In numerous small and extremely painful ways, the conflict was no more comfortable for him than the others; in fact, it was probably more painful for him, as he was changing along with the system.

REFLECTION AND DISCUSSION

➤ Personal Steps to Change

1. Even when a company has a written vision statement, people often argue that they do not know what the vision is. What do they mean?

2. List three roles (such as parent, teacher, manager) in which you are expected to show some leadership.

3. For each entry in Item 2, tell how you are or are not providing a vision.

4. List what you need to do differently in each of your three roles.

➤ Organizational Steps to Change

1. Write a reaction to each of the following:

   "Many senior executives are uncomfortable with the notion of creating and communicating a vision. They have difficulty coming up with anything that is persuasive, exciting, or passionate. There is no life in what they conceptualize."

   "After a lively discussion about their product, I asked, 'Who is willing to die for this vision?' No one spoke up. My question had surprised them and made them somewhat uncomfortable. Why? Because as a politically segmented group, they had executed a rational exercise and formed specific common denominators or generalities into a vision to which no one could object. However, whether undertaken by an individual or a group, a worthwhile vision does not arise from painless compromise. Statements that emerge from such efforts are empty words."

"Many senior people have no idea how to develop a vision and find it very embarrassing to be reminded that their company lacks an adequate vision. As a consequence, it becomes necessary to stop talking about the needs they are not meeting. They implicitly send the message that the issue is no longer discussable. However, sometimes the situation warrants a message that is much more explicit. I know one executive who heard comments from his coworkers almost continuously that they did not know the company's vision. Finally, he met with his top management team, and together they generated a plastic card. Sadly, within a week, the message circulated again, "We don't know the vision." Finally, in frustration, he turned to one of his vice presidents and said, "Go tell them to stop saying that."

"As Gandhi continued speaking, people gradually returned to their seats and began to listen. Why? Because they knew they were hearing something very real, something of great importance. This small, unassuming little man had journeyed through their heartland and captured the essence of who they were. He was now vocalizing it in a way they could feel and understand. Such articulation is often at the heart of radical, deep change. The term radical is derived from the Latin word for 'root.' In mathematics, for example, we use the radical sign to indicate the square root. To make radical change, one must move to the root, the origin or archetype. An influential vision reflects the insight of an individual or group that has deeply contemplated the core issues. Gandhi's vision was such a reflection. It was rooted in both facts and values. It also carried and inspired passion."

2. Reread the section headed "A CEO Finds a Vision." List five of your most important insights.

3. From the section headed "Building Commitment Without a Bread-and-Salt Vision," list three insights that can be usefully employed in your organization.

22

The Power of One

Overcoming our fears and facing the challenges of change can be a painstaking process. To champion our vision, we must be willing to deviate from conventional methods, strive through the seemingly endless series of hurdles and roadblocks, and continue confidently and with courage toward our goal. We must accept the fact that we have the power and the ability to change.

Over the years, I have become a strong believer in the fact that the external world can be changed by altering our internal world. This, however, is not a popular theory. The popular theory is that for a successful change to occur, it must come from the top down, from the outside in. If you want to change the organization, for example, the process must start with the CEO. This is a strongly supported theory and, indeed, the theory of choice among both my colleagues and the managers I meet. I fully acknowledge it as a valid theory. However, I also accept a seemingly opposing theory that postulates that an organization and the world can be changed from the bottom up. One person can make a difference. Consider, by way of example, the story of John Woolman.

John Woolman was an American Quaker who lived in the 1700s. His journal is considered a literary treasure and is still studied in many English classes. His most memorable accomplishment, however, had to do with the process of deep change. During the eighteenth century, many Quakers were wealthy, conservative slave owners. Woolman dedicated his adult life to eliminating the practice of slavery among his brethren.

Woolman pursued this effort by using the art of gentle persuasion. He spent more than twenty years visiting Quakers along the East Coast. He did not criticize people, nor did he make them angry. He merely asked questions like, "What does it mean to be a moral person? What does it mean to own a slave? What does it mean to will a slave over to one's children?" Driven by his vision, he persisted, visiting farm after farm.

By 1770, a century before the Civil War, not one Quaker owned a slave. The Quakers were the first religious group to denounce and renounce slavery. In recounting this story, Robert Greenleaf (1991) points out:

> One wonders what would have been the result if there had been fifty John Woolmans, or even five, traveling the length and breadth of the Colonies in the eighteenth century persuading people, one by one, with gentle non-judgmental argument that a wrong should be righted by individual voluntary action. Perhaps we would not have had the war with its 600,000 casualties and the impoverishment of the South, and with the resultant vexing social problem that is at fever heat 100 years later with no end in sight. We know now, in the perspective of history, that just a slight alleviation of the tension in the 1850s might have avoided the war. A few John Woolmans, just a few, might have made the difference [p. 29]

Woolman hated the idea of slavery and found it intolerable. He was determined to change the minds of his fellow Quakers. His vision, courage, and persistence transformed his church.

There comes a time when we all question whether something is right. At such times, we have to listen and follow our inner voice, even when it means tackling the system and enlisting some unconventional procedures and techniques. One person can make a difference. One person can make deep change in an organization. However, deep change comes at great cost. Enacting change means taking some risks. When we take the necessary risks, we become self-empowered. We begin to better align our internal self with our external world. As our internal power base grows, we become confident and make genuine progress toward our goal. We become energized and slowly begin to recognize that we can make a difference. We begin to understand that one person really can change the system.

➤ Personal Steps to Change

1. When we feel powerless, we usually wait for someone to come along and change our external world. Give a recent example of a time when you felt this way.

2. Why is the theory of change from the bottom up or the inside out less popular than change from the top down or the outside in?

3. Why are both theories valid?

4. What did you learn from the John Woolman story?

5. Identify an issue in your environment that is worth the kind of dedication shown by John Woolman.

➤ Organizational Steps to Change

1. Identify a group in your organization that is waiting for someone to come along and rescue it. Why is the group behaving that way?

2. Describe an incident when you observed an individual trying to change an organization from the bottom up. What did you learn from that incident?

3. If John Woolman worked in your organization, what are some of the issues he might confront?

4. If John Woolman confronted some key issues in your organization, how would he be treated?

5. Why do so few John Woolmans arise in today's organizations?

23

The Power of Many

I once worked with an organization that recognized that the lack of external responsiveness was causing it to become less competitive. The members of the top management team could see that the organization was facing a deep-change-or-slow-death dilemma and decided something must be done. Concluding that they needed to empower their workforce, they made empowerment a top priority in their business plan. A year later, they reviewed their situation and found that they could not identify any action that had been taken to empower their people. Frustrated, they asked me to analyze the situation.

I began by interviewing the twelve most senior people in the organization. I asked them to define empowerment and to tell me how people get empowered. The interviews suggested not a consensus but sharp differences. Their assumptions were divided into two camps.

The managers in the first camp believed that empowerment was about delegation and accountability. Empowerment was a top-down process. They believed that top management should develop a clear vision and then communicate specific plans and assignments to the rest of the management team. Decisions could then be delegated to the lowest appropriate level. Top management would provide the information and resources needed to help people accomplish their tasks. The employees would make the required procedural changes and process improvements, which would generally clarify and simplify their work. The employees would be empowered because they could ask questions and challenge the rules in positive ways.

The other camp believed that empowerment was about risk taking, growth, and change. Empowerment meant trusting people and tolerating their imperfections. When it came to rules, the managers in this group believed that existing structures often presented a barrier to doing what was right. Empowered people were expected to ask for forgiveness rather than permission and would naturally make some mistakes. Organizational members were to become entrepreneurs and risk takers. As result, they would have a sense of ownership and commitment; they would engage in creative conflict, constantly challenging one another, thus exposing and resolving differences and creating a synergy among themselves. This kind of communication and commitment would result in an identification and an alignment with the task.

These two points of view on empowerment are very different. When they were relayed to the management team, there was a heavy silence. Finally, someone with the first view expressed a core concern about the second: "We can't afford loose cannons around here." A person with the second view responded: "When is the last time you saw a cannon of any kind around here?"

It was suddenly very clear why not a single action had been taken on the management team's objective to empower the workforce. Though all the executives assumed that empowerment was good, they had a deep conflict around the meaning and generation process. The first view, what I call the mechanistic approach to empowerment, is summarized in Exhibit 23.1, and the second view, what I call the organic approach, is summarized in Exhibit 23.2.

Empowerment as a Complex Concept

Empowerment is a commonly used buzzword. Everyone is for it. However, problems often arise when we attempt to define the con-

Exhibit 23.1. Mechanistic View of Empowerment.

- Start at the top.

- Develop a clear vision, plans, and assignments.

- Move decisions to the appropriate levels.

- Provide necessary information and resources.

- Encourage process improvement.

In short, empowerment is about *clarity, delegation, control, and accountability.*

Exhibit 23.2. Organic View of Empowerment.

- Start with the needs of the people.

- Expose the difficult issues.

- Model integrity through risk taking.

- Build credibility through small wins.

- Encourage initiative.

- Build teamwork.

In short, empowerment is about *risk, growth, trust, and teamwork.*

cept and begin its implementation in the workplace. As in the last story, differing philosophical assumptions often collide. To determine your own orientation to empowerment, complete both parts of Exhibit 23.3 now.

People usually answer the two parts of Exhibit 23.3 quite differently. This difference suggests that we like the idea of some abstract person having more power. However, when it comes to our subordinates, the more empowered they become, the less comfortable we

Exhibit 23.3. Empowerment: An Exercise.

Part A

Using a scale from 1 (small degree) to 7 (large degree), indicate the extent to which you believe the person in each example is empowered.

Example 1

A middle manager came up with a new system for working with remote locations. The system was a threat to what was currently a highly centralized operation. Careful analysis showed that the change would result in lower cost, increased quality, and better coordination. Furthermore, the individual knew, intuitively, that the change was "right." In making his initial proposals, he received discouraging responses from those above and below. He nevertheless made a long-term commitment to sell his idea slowly.

Example 2

A newly assigned middle manager, attending her first meeting with her new group, listened to a proposal made by her boss. Given her considerable experience with a similar subject at her previous location, she was quite knowledgeable of the shortcomings of the proposal being made. She therefore made a bluntly honest but constructive assessment of the shortcomings in the proposal.

Example 3

A CEO, known to act as a tyrant on occasion, decided that the activities in a certain function should be expanded. The analytical task fell to a middle manager, five layers down in the hierarchy. The manager eventually concluded that the function should be eliminated. His immediate superior told him to "redo" the analysis. After much soul-searching, the man turned in the report recommending the elimination. His superiors then decided that the man would make the presentation directly to the CEO. He agreed to do so.

Example 4

Some years ago, a plant manager was told that a new product must be launched. After an analysis, it was concluded that the only way the project could be accomplished was to promise lifelong employment to the union. This was a radical idea that would clearly not be approved at corporate headquarters or by his direct superior. The plant manager made the promise and proceeded.

Exhibit 23.3. Empowerment: An Exercise, cont'd.

Part B
Now assume that the person in each example is your direct subordinate. Using a scale from 1 (small degree) to 7 (large degree), indicate how comfortable you would be with the actions of the person in each example.

feel. Whereas nearly everyone wants to be more empowered by their boss, fewer people are comfortable with the idea of empowering their subordinates. In other words, though most of us want our bosses to practice the organic model of empowerment, we prefer that our subordinates take the mechanistic approach. When we adhere to this natural preference, we fail to understand something very important about the interrelationship between the two models.

Three Lessons About Empowerment

Several years ago, Gretchen Spreitzer, who is now a professor at the University of Southern California, did an extensive study on empowerment (Spreitzer, 1995, 1996). She focused on three questions: What are the dimensions of empowerment? Does it make a difference if people feel empowered? What are the levers that lead to empowerment in an organization.

The Dimensions of Empowerment

In an analysis of responses from nearly four hundred managers at a Fortune 500 company, Spreitzer was able to identify empirically four dimensions of empowerment:

1. *A sense of meaning.* Their work is important to them; they care about what they are doing.

2. *A sense of competence.* They feel confident about their ability to do the work; they know they can perform.

3. *A sense of self-determination.* They feel free to choose how to do the work; they are not "micromanaged."

4. *A sense of impact.* They feel that they have influence in their unit; people listen to their ideas.

These four dimensions define empowerment. But is empowerment worth all this trouble? Do empowered people perform differently from people who do not have feelings of empowerment?

The Payoffs of Empowerment

Spreitzer found that empowered people see themselves as more innovative than less empowered people see themselves. In addition, both the subordinates and the superiors of empowered people give the empowered people significantly higher scores on measures of innovation.

Empowered people also report having more upward influence. They give themselves higher scores on overall managerial effectiveness, and their subordinates and superiors rate them significantly higher on overall effectiveness. Finally, in terms of actual behavior, people with higher scores on empowerment are more likely to report making second-order or quantum change initiatives than their less empowered counterparts are.

If we want more innovative, more effective, and more influential people in our organizations, empowerment is indeed worth the effort. But this leads us back to my example of the two frustrated groups with different perspectives on how to empower people. Which group was right? The answer to that question depends largely on the individual organization and its own unique set of circumstances.

The Levers of Empowerment

Spreitzer's research also identified four organizational conditions that lead to an empowering environment:

1. *Clear vision and challenge*. Highly empowered people feel that they understand top management's vision for the organization and the strategic direction of the organization and that they have access to the strategic information that they need. They know where the organization is going.

2. *Openness and teamwork*. In their work units, empowered people report a sense of participation, openness, flexibility, concern, creative problem solving, and cohesive teamwork. The unit works together to solve problems.

3. *Discipline and control*. Highly empowered people indicate that in their units, such matters as goals, lines of authority, and task responsibilities are clearly defined.

4. *Support and a sense of security*. Highly empowered people indicate that they receive support from their subordinates, peers, superiors, and others in their work group. They have a sense of secure and predictable relationships.

This list contains a contradiction. On the one hand, conditions 1, 2, and 4 are indicators of an organic perspective. On the other hand, condition 3—discipline and control with clearly defined authority, tasks, and goals—reflects a mechanistic approach. Which is correct?

The answer is that both orientations, organic and mechanistic, are essential and must be considered when developing the structure for an empowering environment. To create an empowering environment, we need to exhibit continuous long-term dedication and management of four dynamic interrelated organizational processes: strategic alignment, clarification of expectations, conflict resolution, and participation and involvement. This kind of effort can be made only by a leader who is empowered.

The Final Key

The four organizational conditions lead to an empowering environment but not to empowerment. In an empowering environment, people are more likely to take risks, experience success, and then feel empowered themselves. We do not, however, empower people. Empowerment cannot be delegated. We can only develop an appropriate empowering environment where people will have to take the initiative to empower themselves. Given this fact, I often ask people at all levels to write answers to the following questions:

1. How can I increase my own sense of meaning and task-alignment?

2. How can I increase my own sense of impact, influence, and power?

3. How can I increase my own sense of competence and confidence to execute?

4. How can I increase my own sense of self-determination and choice?

These are four uncomfortable questions. They shift the responsibility for our empowerment from someone else to ourselves. We all would like to be more empowered. But few of us, when shown what is really involved in becoming empowered, want to pay the price. Ultimately, each of us has exactly as much power as we really want.

REFLECTION AND DISCUSSION

➤ Personal Steps to Change

Write out your answer to each of the four questions in the last section of the text ("The Final Key").

➤ Organizational Steps to Change

Write out your answer to each item in the following question: In attempting to create an empowering environment where others will take the risks that will result in their own growth, empowerment, and connection with the organization, how can I help provide (1) continuous strategic alignment, (2) continuous clarification of expectations, (3) continuous conflict resolution, and (4) continuous participation and involvement?

References

Argyris, C. *Increasing Leadership Effectiveness*. New York: Wiley, 1976.

Argyris, C. *Inner Contradictions of Rigorous Research*. New York: Academic Press, 1980.

Cameron, K. S., and Quinn, R. E. *Diagnosing and Changing Organizational Culture*. San Francisco: Jossey-Bass, 1997.

Campbell, J. *The Hero with a Thousand Faces*. New York: Bollingen Foundation, 1949.

Gordon, A. "The Day at the Beach." *Reader's Digest*, 1960, 76, 79–83.

Greenleaf, R. K. *Servant Leadership: A Journey into the Nature of Legitimate Power and Greatness*. Mahwah, N.J.: Paulist Press, 1991.

Hart, S., and Quinn, R. E. "Roles Executives Play: CEOs, Behavioral Complexity, and Firm Performance." *Human Relations*, 1993, 46.

Kofman, F., and Senge, P. M. "The Heart of Learning Organizations." *Organizational Dynamics*, 1993, XX, 5–21.

McWhinney, W., and Batista, J. "How Remythologizing Can Revitalize Organizations." *Organizational Dynamics*, 1988, 17, 46–58.

Peck, S. *The Road Less Traveled: A New Psychology of Love, Traditional Values, and Spiritual Growth*. New York: Simon & Schuster, 1978.

Penick, H. *Harvey Penick's Little Red Book*. New York: Simon & Schuster, 1992.

Pirsig, R. M. *Zen and the Art of Motorcycle Maintenance*. New York: Morrow, 1974.

Quinn, R. E. *Beyond Rational Management: Mastering the Paradoxes and Competing Demands of High Performance*. San Francisco: Jossey-Bass, 1988.

Quinn, R. E., Faerman, S. R., Thompson, M. P., and McGrath, M. R. *Becoming a Master Manager: A Competency-Based Framework*. (2nd ed.) New York: Wiley, 1996.

Russell, B., and Branch, T. *Second Wind: The Memoir of an Opinionated Man*. New York: Random House, 1979.

Schlesinger, L. A., Eccles, R. G., and Gabarro, J. J. *Management Behavior in Organizations: Texts, Cases, and Readings*. New York: McGraw-Hill, 1983.

Spreitzer, G. "Psychological Empowerment in the Workplace: Dimensions, Measurement, and Validation." *Academy of Management Journal*, 1995, 38(5), 1442–1465.

Spreitzer, G. "Social Structural Antecedents of Workplace Empowerment." *Academy of Management Journal*, 1996, 39(2).

Spreitzer, G., and Quinn, R. E. "Empowering Middle Managers to Be Transformational Leaders." *Journal of Applied Behavioral Science*, Sept. 1996.

Torbert, W. R. *Managing the Corporate Dream: Restructuring for Long-Term Success*. Homewood, Ill.: Dow Jones–Irwin, 1987.

Index